FUN ACT PREP

English & Reading
PRACTICE TESTS
2nd Edition

BECAUSE TEST PREP DOESN'T HAVE TO BE BORING

Mary Kate Mikulskis & Chris Mikulskis

WWW.FUNACTPREP.COM

*ACT® is registered trademark of ACT, Inc. Authors and publisher have no association with ACT, Inc.

Published in the United States of America by CreateSpace

www.funactprep.com

ISBN-13:
978-1515140115

ISBN-10:
1515140113

INTRODUCTION

Students:

We know test prep can be a drag. From spending countless hours navigating massive books, to taking multiple practice tests full of boring subject matter, the drill-and-kill format of typical test prep programs can be mind-numbing. The ACT is a test about *skill*; therefore, why not practice the English and Reading skills you need for success on the ACT, while also reading about sports, music, and popular culture? Let's face it, you might not be learning much if you are bored to tears.

This book contains six practice ACT-like tests—three in English and three in Reading. You can attempt to simulate a real test-taking experience by working on an entire test in one sitting (give yourself 45 minutes to answer 75 English questions and 35 minutes to answer 40 reading questions), or work on a passage or two at a time. Take your time and review your answers after each chunk you work on and take note of what skills you have down and which you struggle with. Focus on the skills that are giving you problems with more practice, textbooks, your teacher, or *Fun ACT Prep: Skill by Skill.* Work hard but also lighten up and have fun!

Teachers & Parents:

Test prep is a serious topic. High-stakes tests put pressure on students, parents, and teachers alike. Many teachers feel an obligation to prepare students for standardized tests, but struggle to keep students' attention with the same old materials. Parents often invest in dense test prep books and expensive programs only to find their children less than thrilled to participate.

As high school English teachers, we believe that rigor does not have to equal boredom. One key to helping students improve their English and Reading skills is to get them engaged in the material. By incorporating subjects relevant to teens' lives, this book encourages reluctant students and reinvigorates more motivated learners.

This book is not all fun and games, though; behind the teen-friendly content are questions modeled very closely after the ACT. With years of test preparation experience, we know the types of questions the ACT is likely to ask, the skills it emphasizes, and the curveballs it throws students. And we have witnessed students' enthusiasm to engage in test preparation when using these materials in our own classrooms.

This book can be used as part of the English/Reading curriculum, for a supplemental test preparation program, or for students' independent use.

Test 1

ENGLISH

75 questions

45 minutes

ANSWER SHEET- ENGLISH TEST 1

1._____	16._____	31._____	46._____	61._____
2._____	17._____	32._____	47._____	62._____
3._____	18._____	33._____	48._____	63._____
4._____	19._____	34._____	49._____	64._____
5._____	20._____	35._____	50._____	65._____
6._____	21._____	36._____	51._____	66._____
7._____	22._____	37._____	52._____	67._____
8._____	23._____	38._____	53._____	68._____
9._____	24._____	39._____	54._____	69._____
10._____	25._____	40._____	55._____	70._____
11._____	26._____	41._____	56._____	71._____
12._____	27._____	42._____	57._____	72._____
13._____	28._____	43._____	58._____	73._____
14._____	29._____	44._____	59._____	74._____
15._____	30._____	45._____	60._____	75._____

Gaga for Gaga

Whether dressed in bubbles, Beanie Babies, or raw beef, Lady Gaga never fails to make an impression. Lady Gaga **(1)was not born—she was made,** an example of the power of individuality and reinvention.

The iconic pop star had humble beginnings. Stefani Germonatta was born in New York City in 1986. Her fans may be surprised to learn that the attention-grabbing singer attended a strict Catholic school. After graduation, she enrolled in the prestigious Tisch School for the Performing Arts at New York University. Her music career, however, started much earlier: **(2)Germonatta began playing the piano at age four and wrote her first song at age thirteen.**

Germonatta performed **(3)solo and on her own** at open-mikes around New York City, but her first official career in the music industry was as a songwriter **(4) she wrote for acts** like the Pussycat Dolls, New Kids on the Block, Fergie, and Britney Spears. Singer Akon recognized her vocal talents when she sang a song she wrote for him; he **(5)became** instrumental in helping her land her own recording deal. By 2007, Germanotta had

1. Which of the following expressions would NOT reflect a contrast in ideas?

   A. NO CHANGE
   B. was not only born, but also was made,
   C. was not born; instead, she became
   D. was not born, but rather was made,

2. If the underlined statement were omitted, the passage would primarily lose:

   F. a detail that informs readers of the length of the singer's "career."
   G. an indication of Lady Gaga's age.
   H. an irrelevant detail that distracts from the focus of the paragraph.
   J. information about Lady Gaga's education.

3.   A. NO CHANGE
    B. unaccompanied, by herself,
    C. independently
    D. autonomously and alone

4.   F. NO CHANGE
    G. and she wrote for acts
    H. ,where she was a songwriter for acts
    J. writing for acts

5. Which of the following options would NOT be acceptable?

   A. NO CHANGE
   B. would become
   C. becoming
   D. later became

transformed herself **(6), a moniker inspired by the Queen song "Radio Ga Ga,"** into Lady Gaga. Her debut album **(7)*The Fame*** lived up to its name, making Gaga an overnight sensation. Soon everyone was talking about "Gaga." **(8)Instant hits like "Just Dance" and "Poker Face" climbing up the charts and dominating the airwaves.**

(9)In addition to her catchy pop tunes, Gaga's unique style captivates her fans. Gaga's distinctive look is the result of a collaboration among her designers, stylists, hair and makeup team, and artists, **(10)who work** together in a group known as Haus of Gaga. Gaga explains that music is only part of the package **(11) : She** sees her role as not merely a singer, but as a performance artist.

[1]Her first single from her follow-up to *The Fame*, **(12) titled "Born This Way,"** became the fastest-downloaded song ever on iTunes. [2]Gaga refers to her fans as her "little monsters" and is an advocate for self-expression and individuality. [3]**(13)Despite this criticism,** Lady Gaga continues to shine in the spotlight

6. The best placement for the underlined portion would be
   F. where it is now.
   G. after the word *Germanotta*
   H. after the word *Gaga* (replacing the second comma with a period)
   J. before the phrase *By 2007* (lowercasing *by*)

7. A. NO CHANGE
   B. , *The Fame*,
   C. called *The Fame*
   D. OMIT the underlined portion

8. F. NO CHANGE
   G. Instant hits like "Just Dance" and "Poker Face" were climbing up the charts and dominated the airwaves.
   H. Climbing up the charts and dominating the airwaves were "Just Dance" and "Poker Face," instant hits.
   J. Instant hits like "Just Dance" and "Poker Face" climbed up the charts and dominated the airwaves.

9. A. NO CHANGE
   B. Regardless of
   C. In spite of
   D. Plus

10. F. NO CHANGE
    G. whom work
    H. who are working
    J. whom have worked

11. Which of the following changes would NOT be acceptable?
    A. because she
    B. ; she
    C. since she
    D. although she

12. F. NO CHANGE
    G. which she named "Born This Way"
    H. referred to as "Born This Way,"
    J. "Born This Way,"

13. The underlined portion can be placed everywhere EXCEPT:
    A. where it is now
    B. after the name *Lady Gaga* (lowercasing *despite*)
    C. after the word *to* and before the word *shine* (lowercasing *despite*)
    D. after the word *spotlight* (lowercasing *despite*)

without experiencing a sophomore

slump. [4]Her critics, however, argue that she

is not unique, namely because her music and

outlandish style draw many comparisons to

'90s-era Madonna. **[14]**

Lady Gaga has redefined what it means to be a

female pop star, paving the way for more theatrics and

breaking the mold for generations of performers to

come. **[15]**

14. Which of the following sequences of sentences makes this paragraph most logical?

    F. NO CHANGE
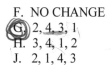
    G. 2, 4, 3, 1
    H. 3, 4, 1, 2
    J. 2, 1, 4, 3

15. Suppose the writer was considering adding the following true statement:

She has spawned imitators like Ke$ha and Nicki Minaj, but there will never be another Gaga.

Should the writer make this addition?

    A. YES, because Nicki Minaj and Ke$ha are famous performers.
    B. YES, because it provides examples of the extent of Gaga's influence on the music industry.
    C. NO, because these artists are very different from Gaga.
    D. NO, because it strays from the focus of the essay.

PASSAGE II

The Celebrity Blogger Celebrity

[1]

(16)While Perez Hilton's snarky image was part of his popularity. This incident led many people to view him as a hypocrite, as he had chastised other celebrities for using the same slurs **(17)(Hilton's criticism of *Grey's Anatomy* actor Isaiah Washington's use of the same term led to Washington's termination from the popular television series)**. The backlash led Hilton to do something out of character—offer an apology. Soon after, Hilton made another shocking announcement: *PerezHilton.com* would become a tolerant, hate-free website. **(18)Hilton realized that the vile epithets that made him famous served as a bad example for his audience.**

[2]

(19)Nowadays, *PerezHilton.com* still serves up juicy celebrity gossip, and Hilton shares his opinion, but he is much gentler when discussing the struggles of celebrities, whether in their careers or personal lives. Hilton may have come to realize the **(20) pressure and strain** under which celebrities live since he has become

16. F. NO CHANGE
    G. While Perez Hilton's snarky image was part of his popularity, and this incident
    H. While Perez Hilton's snarky image was part of his popularity, this incident
    J. While Perez Hilton's snarky image was part of his popularity; this incident

17. The writer is considering deleting the underlined statement. The statement should be:

    A. KEPT, because it speaks to Hilton's ability to tell celebrities what to do.
    B. KEPT, because it serves as an example of Hilton's hypocrisy when it comes to people using derogatory terms.
    C. DELETED, because *Grey's Anatomy* has nothing to do with Hilton's website.
    D. DELETED, because Isaiah Washington is not as famous as other celebrities Hilton writes about on his site.

18. F. NO CHANGE
    G. Realizing that vile epithets made him famous, Hilton served as a bad example for his audience.
    H. The vile epithets that made him famous were a bad example for Hilton's audience.
    J. Hilton realized that the vile epithets that had made him famous badly served as examples for his audience.

19. A. NO CHANGE
    B. Recently,
    C. Consequently,
    D. Therefore,

20. F. NO CHANGE
    G. scrutiny
    H. forcible weight
    J. anxious angst

4

a celebrity himself. In addition to the millions of daily visitors to his **(21)site, Hilton** has a national audience on his syndicated radio spots and appears on television programs and in magazines and music videos. His site includes pictures of him posing with celebrities at star-studded events, walking the red carpet with the same newsmakers who have **(22)unintentional** helped to thrust him into the spotlight.

[3]

Fame and fortune used to be the fate of only movie stars and singing sensations. However, now **(23)the people who write** about the rich and famous are celebrities themselves, **(24)thanks to** the rise of **(25)the internet, paparazzi photography, and celebrity bloggers.** The most notorious celebrity blogger is Perez Hilton. Hilton went from being a struggling actor **(26)virtually overnight** to the writer of a successful website. *PerezHilton.com* gained attention for

21. A. NO CHANGE
    B. site; Hilton
    C. site—Hilton
    D. site Hilton

22. F. NO CHANGE
    G. in an inadvertent manner
    H. somewhat accidentally
    J. OMIT the underlined portion

23. All of the following choices would be acceptable EXCEPT:

    A. NO CHANGE
    B. the people whom writing
    C. those who write
    D. the people writing

24. Which option would NOT be acceptable?

    F. NO CHANGE
    G. due to
    H. as a result of
    J. despite

25. A. NO CHANGE
    B. websites, the paparazzi, and posts on blogs.
    C. the internet, the paparazzi, and blogs.
    D. people going on websites, reading blogs, and paparazzi photography.

26. The underlined portion should be placed:
    F. where it is now.
    G. after the word *website* (moving the period to the end of the sentence).
    H. after the word *being.*
    J. after the word *writer.*

5

displaying pictures of celebrities **(27)covered with**

crude doodles and nasty comments created by Hilton.

27. If the underlined portion were deleted, the passage would primarily lose:

    A. imagery of the content on Hilton's site.
    B. an explanation of the popularity and criticism Hilton's site received.
    C. a detail that explains the revenue-generating power of the website.
    D. an irrelevant comment that distracts from the focus of the paragraph. X

[4]

Such negativity earned Perez many enemies who

felt insulted by the personal attacks he launched on

them. Hilton's verbal abuse **(28)surpassed** the web

when one of his regular targets, singer will.i.am of the

Black Eyed Peas, confronted Hilton about **(29)his**

harassment of band mate Fergie. Perez responded by

calling will.i.am a derogatory term, and soon, the assault

became physical. **[30]**

28. Which of the following choices would NOT be acceptable?

    F. transcended
    G. rose beyond
    H. amplified
    J. exceeded

29. The pronoun *his* refers to:

    A. Hilton
    B. will.i.am
    C. the Black Eyed Peas
    D. Fergie

30. The most logical order of paragraphs is:

    F. NO CHANGE
    G. 4, 2, 1, 3
    H. 3, 4, 1, 2
    J. 3, 4, 2, 1

Designer Dogs

Designer duds carry a lot of status.(31) One

unexpected status symbol **(32)that has gained**

popularity is the designer dog. Pet owners are choosing

pooches carefully **(33)and** providing man's best friend

with the best that life has to offer.

While rescuing dogs from shelters is a noble

(34)cause many dog owners prefer to customize their

pets. Take the case of **(35)Big Splash the** world's most

expensive dog. The Tibetan mastiff sold for 1.5 million

dollars. This is no ordinary dog: Big Splash comes from

an impressive lineage of highly regarded canines and

(36)was the same breed owned by legends like Genghis

Khan and Gandhi. Big Splash may end up being a

lucrative investment on his 1.5 million dollar price tag,

(37)marked by his fiery red fur, as it is likely that his

offspring will fetch an equally impressive price.

31. The author wishes to add the following statement after sentence 1 (removing the period):
    —*watches, cars, jeans, and gym shoes are often selected carefully by their owners to convey a certain image.*

    Should the author add this statement?
    A. YES, because it provides examples of status symbols.
    B. YES, because it shows items people value more than pets.
    C. NO, because this passage is about dogs, not objects.
    D. NO, because these items carry a higher status than pets.

32.   F. NO CHANGE
        G. that is gaining
        H. gaining
        J. that has grown

33.   A. NO CHANGE
        B. but
        C. yet
        D. ;however,

34.   F. NO CHANGE
        G. cause—
        H. cause, and
        J. cause,

35.   A. NO CHANGE
        B. Big Splash who is the
        C. Big Splash, the
        D. Big Splash; the

36.   F. NO CHANGE
        G. has been
        H. is
        J. were

37. The best placement for the underlined portion is:
    A. where it is now
    B. at the end of the sentence (replacing the comma with a period).
    C. at the beginning of the sentence (capitalizing the word *marked*).
    D. after the word *offspring* (offset with commas).

7

Dog lovers do not have to spend millions of dollars **(38), however;** in order to own a customized breed. Dog breeders have been developing **(39)unusual and unique** varieties **(40) these have been designed** to contain the best attribute of each purebred breed. For instance, those looking for a tiny dog to tote around might **(41)seek out** a Snorkie (miniature schnauzer/Yorkshire terrier mix), while people preferring a larger, more rugged dog might choose a Pitweiler (Pitbull/Rottweiler mix).

In addition to breed, many dogs are accessorized better than the most glamorous humans. **(42)For example, pop star Jessica Simpson could often be seen carrying her beloved maltipoo Daisy around in a Louis Vuitton dog carrier (estimated retail price: $2100).** Crystal collars, pink tutus, and custom-made tuxedos and ball gowns are just a few of the garments readily available for dogs to don. Pampered pups can show off **(43) its** style at doggie day care centers, spas, and hotels. There are canine yoga classes and massage services to promote much-needed rest and relaxation

38. F. NO CHANGE
    G. ; however,
    H. , however,
    J. –however—

39. A. NO CHANGE
    B. unusual and peculiar
    C. unusual and most peculiar
    D. unusual and more unique

40. F. NO CHANGE
    G. which have been designed
    H. designed
    J. having been designed

41. A. NO CHANGE
    B. want to buy for themselves
    C. beg for
    D. hunt

42. The writer is considering deleting the underlined portion. If so, the passage would primarily lose:

    F. a relevant example to support the paragraph's main idea
    G. a detail about famous dog owners
    H. an unnecessary diversion from the topic of designer dogs
    J. a snobbish reference only fashion-oriented people would understand

43. A. NO CHANGE
    B. it's
    C. they're
    D. their

(44)for pets leading a stressful lifestyle.

(45) Therefore, the statement "It's a dog's life" has

taken on a whole new meaning.

44. Which of the following placements of the underlined portion would NOT be acceptable?

    F. where it is now
    G. after the word *promote*
    H. at the beginning of the sentence (capitalizing the first word and inserting a comma)
    J. after the word *services*

45. A. NO CHANGE
    B. However,
    C. All in all,
    D. That's why,

Sweet for Sugar

Head pounding, Lucy searched the house wildly, throwing open cabinets **(46)while she rummaged through drawers.** Nothing. "Relax," she told herself. "You don't really want some. It's not good for you. Take a deep breath and let the craving pass." It was no use. Her habit consumed her daily for as long as she could remember, and trying to break her addiction **(47)had proved** more difficult than she thought. The withdrawal symptoms as her body tried to adjust to the lack of the stimulant **(48), not to mention the emotional ups and downs,** were almost unbearable. She just couldn't go one more minute without it: sugar.

Sure, lots of people liked dessert or the occasional dish of ice cream, but Lucy was different. **(49)Jokingly referring to** sugar as "Vitamin S," somehow sweets had become a regular part of her life. **(50)Was it just a coincidence, she reflected, that her first job as a teenager had been at a candy shop?** Perhaps she was unknowingly drawn to the job due to her propensity for sweets.

46. F. NO CHANGE
     G. rummaging through drawers.
     H. and rummaging through drawers.
     J. and she also looked through drawers.

47. A. NO CHANGE
     B. was proving
     C. proved
     D. would have proved

48. The author is considering omitting the underlined statement. Should she make this change?

     F. YES, because it is not scientifically proven.
     G. YES, because the sentence is too long and difficult to read.
     H. NO, because it makes the story relatable to the audience.
     J. NO, because it highlights the psychological, as well as physical, effects of sugar withdrawal.

49. A. NO CHANGE
     B. As a joke, she referred to
     C. She thought it was funny that she called
     D. Although she referred to

50. The writer intends to show that the main character's sweet tooth is an ingrained quality. Which of the following sentences supports this idea?

     F. NO CHANGE
     G. Her colleagues at the office left candy dishes out on their desks, which she helped herself to often.
     H. Her students often brought her apples and other treats, she realized.
     J. Lucy thought that working at a dentist's office would help her break her habit of eating candy and drinking soda.

Luckily, Lucy did not have a weight problem **(51)because she allocated** a large portion of her diet to sugar, her weight was healthy. **(52) Although** she realized that as she got older, this would likely change, and besides, even if she looked healthy on the outside, **(53)whom knew** how all that sugar **(54)effects herself** on the inside.

Lucy decided to purge her cabinets of the substance **(55)making a conscious effort to rid sugar from her life**. The task was easier said than done, however: **(56)Obviously**, the candy bars, cookies, and tubs of frosting had to go, but as she looked carefully at the ingredient labels of the items in the **(57)pantry Lucy** was surprised to find sugar in more unexpected places, including barbeque sauce, certain crackers, and even seemingly healthy foods like yogurt, orange juice, and tomato soup. **[58]**

51. A. NO CHANGE
    B. and because she allowed
    C. ; despite allocating
    D. ; on the other hand, she reserved

52. F. NO CHANGE
    G. While
    H. However,
    J. On the other hand,

53. A. NO CHANGE
    B. who knew
    C. whoever knows
    D. whomever knows

54. F. NO CHANGE
    G. would of ended up affecting her
    H. could effect her body
    J. was affecting her

55. The best placement for the underlined portion is:
    A. where it is now
    B. after the word *purge* (offset on each side with commas)
    C. at the beginning of the sentence (capitalizing *making* and adding a comma after *life*)
    D. OMIT the underlined portion.

56. Which of the following choices would NOT be appropriate?
    F. Of course,
    G. Frankly,
    H. Clearly,
    J. Undoubtedly,

57. A. NO CHANGE
    B. pantry; Lucy
    C. pantry but Lucy
    D. pantry, Lucy

58. The author is considering adding the following information:
No wonder Americans today eat an average of 32 pounds of sugar a year!

Should the author make this addition?

    F. YES, because it highlights Lucy's surprise at finding hidden sugars in unexpected foods.
    G. YES, because it tells the reader exactly how much sugar Lucy eats in a year.
    H. NO, because the data is unreliable and not scientific.
    J. NO, because the statement becomes irrelevant if the main character is not American.

The next day, Lucy committed to a day of low-sugar eating. Instead of reaching for a bowl of sugary cereal, she prepared a healthy egg white omelet with vegetables. In place of the usual soda pop with lunch, she substituted a glass of water with lemon. After dinner, **(59)while** she normally would crave a slice of pie or homemade cookie, Lucy had some fresh fruit. Although she developed uncomfortable afflictions **(60)headache, fatigue, and mood swings** these physical symptoms made Lucy realize just how dependent she had become on sugar. She toughed it out, and after about a week, she felt better than ever. She even began to crave, of all things, vegetables!

59. A. NO CHANGE
     B. and
     C. when
     D. as

60. All of the following replacements for the underlined portion would be acceptable EXCEPT:

     F. : headache, fatigue, and mood swings
     G. —headache, fatigue, and mood swings—
     H. (headache, fatigue, and mood swings),
     J. , including headache, fatigue, and mood swings,

Pants on the Ground

Everyone knows that speeding or jaywalking can lead to fines and tickets. But now, people may want to make sure that their pants are not breaking the law. In 2007, the town of Delcambre, Louisiana, made sagging pants illegal; **(61)violators** now face a $500 fine. Since then, other towns across the United States have followed suit. Lawmakers claim that the fashion is **(62) linked to and associated with** juvenile delinquency, and the exposure of underwear violates public decency laws. However, opponents believe that such laws restrict individual freedom and are **(63)discriminatory**.

[1]

Sagging pants were first made popular by hip-hop artists in the 1990s. The trend made a resurgence a decade later and became more widespread. **(64)More recently, while sagging pants used to be found predominantly in music videos and urban communities, sagging pants have been donned by teens and young adults of all races, classes, and regions**. What many "saggers" may not **(65) realize; though** is that this trend has a less than fashionable

61. Which of the following alternatives to the underlined portion would NOT fit the tone of this essay?
    A. lawbreakers
    B. perps
    C. offenders
    D. wrongdoers

62. F. NO CHANGE
    G. related with
    H. associated with
    J. connected to and inspired from

63. The author wishes to convey the view that these laws unfairly target certain segments of the population. The word that would convey this the LEAST is:

    A. discriminatory
    B. bigoted
    C. stereotypical
    D. prejudiced

64. F. NO CHANGE
    G. While sagging pants used to be found predominantly in music videos and urban communities, sagging pants have now been donned by teens and young adults of all races, classes, and regions.
    H. Predominantly found in music videos and urban communities, teens and young adults of all races, classes, and regions have donned sagging pants.
    J. Teens and young adults of all races, classes, and regions, predominantly found in music videos and urban communities, have donned sagging pants.

65. A. NO CHANGE
    B. realize—though—
    C. realize, though
    D. realize, though,

13

origin: Prison inmates inadvertently let their jailhouse pants sag **(66)because they were not allowed to wear belts.**

[2]

Just as students have tried to get around dress code restrictions, schools have had to get **(67)creatively ingenious** in regulating sagging pants. A school in Tennessee, for example, decided to use humor to address a somewhat serious issue. Students wearing saggy pants were issued zip ties to hold up their pants,**(68) which were displayed on a bulletin board.** The school called this process "Getting Urkeled" **(69) (a reference to the high-pants-and-suspenders-wearing character Steve Urkel from the 1990s sitcom *Family Matters*).**

[3]

Other opponents of sagging pants are finding different ways to get their message out. A billboard in New York proclaimed, "Raise Your Image. Raise Your Pants," while bus riders in Fort Worth, Texas, were told, "Pull 'em up or find another ride." Even President Obama spoke out against the fashion, telling MTV, "Brothers should pull up their pants."

66. The best placement of the underlined portion is:

    F. NO CHANGE
    G. before the word *prison*
    H. before the word *inadvertently*
    J. OMIT the underlined portion

67. A. NO CHANGE
    B. artistically inventive
    C. imaginative
    D. serious

68. F. NO CHANGE
    G. and they were displayed on a bulletin board.
    H. displaying them on a bulletin board.
    J. and their pictures were displayed on a bulletin board.

69. If the underlined portion were deleted, the passage would primarily lose:

    A. an explanation of the term *Urkeled.*
    B. an explanation of the origin of the sagging pants trend.
    C. an irrelevant detail about old sitcoms.
    D. a justification for the school's policy.

This connection to criminals may be one of the reasons why so many adults **(70)are grossed out by** this fashion statement. Others, **(71)though**, simply do not like the blatant display of undergarments. Some students, in order to get around school dress codes banning sagging pants, have adapted the style, displaying basketball shorts underneath their pants **(72)instead of** actual underwear.

Perhaps the most famous anti-sag activist is "General" Larry Platt, **(73)his** performance of his own original song, "Pants on the Ground" on *American Idol,* became an overnight sensation. The 62-year old's anthem was downloaded over 150,000 times on iTunes and was viewed over ten million times on YouTube. Chances are, the outrage over sagging pants will subside just as disdain of bare ankles, long hair on men, and facial jewelry has faded over time.   In the

70.   F. NO CHANGE
      G. are appalled by
      H. want to gag
      J. squirm at the sight of

71. Which of the alternatives to the underlined portion would NOT be acceptable?
      A. however,
      B. meanwhile,
      C. consequently,
      D. on the other hand,

72. All of the alternatives to the underlined portion are acceptable EXCEPT:

      F. rather than
      G. despite
      H. as an alternative to
      J. in place of

73.   A. NO CHANGE
      B. that
      C. which
      D. whose

meantime **(74) just to play it safe,** it might be best to

74. All of the following corrections to the underlined portion would be acceptable EXCEPT:

F. just to play it safe
G. (just to play it safe),
H. —just to play it safe—
J. , just to play it safe,

wear a belt to avoid breaking any laws. [75]

75 . For the sake of logic and coherence, the best order of the body paragraphs is:

A. NO CHANGE
B. 1, 4, 2, 3
C. 1, 3, 2, 4
D. 3, 2, 1, 4

END OF ENGLISH TEST 1

Test 1

READING

40 questions

35 minutes

ANSWER SHEET-READING TEST 1

1.____   11.____   21.____   31.____

2.____   12.____   22.____   32.____

3.____   13.____   23.____   33.____

4.____   14.____   24.____   34.____

5.____   15.____   25.____   35.____

6.____   16.____   26.____   36.____

7.____   17.____   27.____   37.____

8.____   18.____   28.____   38.____

9.____   19.____   29.____   39.____

10.____   20.____   30.____   40.____

PASSAGE I—PROSE FICTION   "The Perfect Date"

"What did I even do wrong?" Justin asked himself silently. "Now I'm starting to understand the old cliché, 'nice guys finish last.'" He shuffled away self-consciously from the dim porch light of her house into
5 the clear blackness enveloping him. He was now hyper-aware of his appearance: His awkward movement from the porch, his poor posture as he hung his head, and the way his toes pointed slightly inward from step to step. What if she were watching from the window, dissecting
10 his gait? How embarrassing.

Justin was raised with proper morals; he was truly a gentleman tonight, just as his mom had advised. He picked up his date, opened the car door for her, paid for dinner and the movie, took her back home before her
15 curfew, and didn't expect anything more than a genuine smile, hug, or an "I-really-had-fun-with-you-tonight." Sure, deep down he longed for their eyes to lock, leading to that perfect, first kiss, but that was wishful thinking. Any show of affection would have been better than the
20 reality of the whispered, "Bye, Justin. Thanks," and the gentle swipe on the shoulder from her long blond hair when she sharply turned to grab her screen door to escape his company.

They really had a great time. This was a fact
25 Justin wasn't creating subconsciously to protect his ego. They radiated matching genuine smiles when he came to pick her up. They talked in the car about their mutual love of pop songs and listened on the way to dinner. They laughed and laughed over dinner as they regaled
30 stories of old Mrs. Shulter, their junior English teacher, and her famous cat sweaters and her favorite angry shout, "Stifle yourself!" His date even snorted from laughing so hard. At the movie, he thought about putting his arm around her like he'd seen in so many TV shows
35 and movies where so many suave guys pull the old "yawn move" and stretch their arms around their dates' shoulders (naturally the girls snuggle in close and sigh dreamily). Justin decided against both, thinking that she would appreciate his respectfulness—or was it that he
40 was too shy to try? Justin sighed and pulled his car keys from his jeans' pocket as he continued in the dark toward his parked car. The porch light went out behind him.

The car keys' jingling seemed to awaken a single cricket from the hedge off to the side. Two pigeon-
45 toed steps later, though, a cacophony of laughter from the hidden multitude of insects violated the solemnity of the moment. Had the springtime crickets noticed his failure too? Had they held their breath when the teenagers passed by on the way up to the front porch? Did they

50 gasp when she shrank away into the house without any show of affection? The sound was becoming obnoxious. If crickets could laugh at him, he could only imagine how mortified he would feel on Monday at school. "Might as well get used to it," he thought to himself.
55 "She's going to tell everyone about how awful of a date this was and everyone at school's going to laugh, too." Justin picked up the pace and manipulated his car alarm remote in the dark. The sharp double-beep seemed to silence the heckling audience. There was nothing more
60 he wanted than to ride away from her house and forget the whole humiliating episode that took place only moments ago.

Justin popped the car door open and sank into the driver's seat. He found the car key and attempted to
65 calm his shaking hand with a deep breath in order to slide the key into the ignition. He cranked the engine and heard the brief whine and anxious roar. He was more than ready to abandon the scene of his failure, and with it, he had to change that pop radio station. Justin fumbled
70 with the buttons of his radio, settling on an '80s station. "Could the world be any more cruel and heartless?" he thought as the singer cried out, "You comin' back to me is against all odds..." Nothing was letting him sever the memories of disappointment of the date and himself.

75 Just as Justin reached to put the car in gear and certainly never return, he was startled by sudden taps at the window. His downtrodden heart received a jolt and raced to life. It was her—she had come back! He looked through the window and instinctively smiled like a tod-
80 dler on his birthday waiting to blow out the candles of his cake. She gracefully smiled back. He somehow found the window switch even though his furiously trembling hands seemed to fight him. The window rolled down slower than it had ever done before. He didn't know
85 what to expect, but just her coming back to his car meant everything to him. "I just want to say," she whispered through her smile, "that I had a really nice time tonight." Justin felt his ears getting red—his personalized display of nerves. Thankfully it was too dark for her to notice
90 another one of his flaws. Justin squeaked, "Uhh, me too." His eyes wanted look away thanks to yet another humiliation, but before they got their way, he felt a gentle touch on the back of his neck. She leaned into the window, her eyes slowly closing. He didn't think. He let
95 his eyes close and felt her soft lips touch his. His heart pounded. He didn't want this moment to end, but it did, just as fast as it had started. She broke contact and pulled away with a giggle only an angel could sound. She was gone, jetting away in front of his car, the headlights re-

100 vealing her sprint. Justin tried to watch every movement,
but the night sky only allowed him glimpses of a bob-
bing shadow against the background of her house. She
scurried inside and closed the door. Justin could not wipe
the smile from his face. He couldn't wait to see her again
105 and wished for her to come right back out of the door,
but she didn't—that was okay, though. All was right
with the world. Justin faced forward, put the car in gear,
and replayed the moment in his head until sleep took
hold hours later.

110   "Maybe nice guys don't finish last," Justin con-
cluded while lying in his bed, his heart still pounding.

1. The passage suggests that Justin is concerned with all of
the following EXCEPT:

    A. acting in a courteous manner toward his date.
    B. not disappointing his parents.
    C. what his peers will think about the date.
    D. the annoying sound of the insects.

2. The passage as a whole best supports which of the
following explanations for Justin's inability to give his
date a kiss at her doorstep?

    F. He was embarrassed of all the little things he had
done wrong throughout the night.
    G. He was self-conscious of his own body image and
movements.
    H. His anxiety about the kiss prevented his action.
    J. His shy but well-mannered behavior hindered his
forward advances.

3. It is implied in the fourth paragraph (lines 43-62) that
Justin imagines all of the following EXCEPT:

    A. his date ridiculing him to others.
    B. an audience jeering.
    C. crickets quietly observing the daters' advance to
the house.
    D. his date running back out to meet him.

4. It can be reasonably inferred that Justin's date:

    F. managed to control her own skittishness before
Justin left.
    G. came back out and kissed him out of pity.
    H. ran away from the car due to Justin's poor kissing
ability.
    J. kissed him so that he did not spread rumors about
her at school.

5. The statement, "she sharply turned to grab the screen
door to escape his company" (lines 22-23), serves the
story by:

    A. enhancing the tension between the two characters.
    B. emphasizing the narrator's view of the situation.
    C. indicating her need to avoid letting her parents
glimpse an intimate moment.
    D. demonstrating her desire to hurry and check her
breath.

6. The author would most likely agree with which of the
following statements?

    F. Nice guys don't always finish last.
    G. A first date should not include any romance.
    H. Dating is a rite of passage for many teenagers.
    J. Chivalry is not dead.

7. It can be reasonably inferred from the passage that the
reason why Justin must change the radio station (line 69)
is because:

    A. he prefers '80s music to pop music.
    B. he felt the need to rid his mind of everything about
the date.
    C. he wanted to sulk in his misery with a sad song.
    D. he suddenly despised pop music only because his
date enjoyed it.

8. Until the start of the sixth paragraph, Justin's attitude
toward the date is most likely one of:

    F. confusion.
    G. spite.
    H. understanding.
    J. apathy.

9. The only information the passage provides about Justin's
school is that:

    A. he is currently performing poorly in English.
    B. the teachers at the school frequently yell at the stu-
dents.
    C. the students at the school are quick to judge others.
    D. both he and his date have a teacher in common.

10. The author most likely includes information about suave
guys on TV shows and movies (lines 35-38) in order to:

    F. describe what a female anticipates when at a mov-
ie.
    G. emphasize Justin's lack of knowledge of proper
dating decorum.
    H. contrast glorified male behavior with that of Jus-
tin's.
    J. highlight inappropriate behavior propagated by the
media.

PASSAGE II—SOCIAL SCIENCE "McDonald's Worldwide"

One of the most famous symbols around the world is the iconic golden arches. Like its logo, McDonald's menu items are just as recognizable. Who doesn't know the Big Mac, Quarter Pounder, or Egg McMuffin?
5   Though most customers have grown accustomed to seeing regular items on the menu boards, McDonald's continuously markets new menu items for the changing tastes of its customers. For example, salads, apple slices, and Fruit and Yogurt Parfaits, though relatively recent additions to
10 McDonald's menus compared to some of the classics, reflect the customers' desires. Its willingness to meet the demands and cravings of its clientele helps make McDonald's a permanent fixture in major cities and small towns. The company knows the value of these different tastes,
15 and in efforts to please its patrons, the restaurant chain has provided and continues to offer some unique food items in various regions across the U.S. and the world.

It may not be too far of a stretch for some to embrace the Cajun McChicken Sandwich all over the U.S.
20 This burger is a standard McChicken sandwich with Cajun spices produced occasionally in the Southern regions of the U.S. Also not straying far from standard menu items is the Texas Homestyle Burger, which consists of a quarter pound beef patty with lettuce, tomato, pickle, and
25 onion, but with an increased amount of mustard. However, other regional items may be a bit more surprising to the casual McDonald's visitor. Visit certain Wisconsin restaurants for their seasonal bratwurst value meal or Maryland and Delaware for their crab cakes. Grab a
30 Green Chile Double Cheeseburger in New Mexico or a McLobster in the northeastern United States. Though some of these menu items may appeal to the palate of certain regions of customers, the international variations change drastically from country to country based on
35 tastes, cultural, or religious reasons, all of which McDonald's holds vital.

International tastes require an international menu; what McDonald's does with this knowledge determines a great deal for its bottom line as it continues to
40 grow worldwide. A food staple in Asian countries, rice is offered in McDonald's restaurants in the form of McRice, but only consisting of ordinary brown rice. Pork burgers are featured as a normal part of the menu in Hong Kong, but some seasonal items include the Shogun Burger (a
45 pork bun served with Teriyaki sauce) and pineapple or red bean sundaes. In Korea, McDonald's chains serve shrimp and *bulgogi* burgers (thinly sliced marinated beef) and McWings, a chicken wing menu item. Taiwanese restaurants prepare *fan kao*, a burger-like item with rice patties
50 in place of buns.

North of the American border in French-speaking provinces, poutine is featured, which consists of French fries and cheese curds covered in brown gravy. In South America, Brazilian restaurants serve the McCala-
55 bresa, a spicy pepperoni patty with a vinaigrette (a mixture of oil and vinegar flavored with spices). Veggie burgers, though not as peculiar to the American palate as other international meals, exist in restaurants where there is a demand for them, such as in India or Western Europe.
60 Indian chains supply more than just the McVeggie Burger, though, in order to satisfy a mainly non-meat eating culture. Based on these cultural and religious beliefs, Indian McDonald's restaurants do not serve beef or pork items.

65 The Maharaja Mac is like the Big Mac but with two spiced chicken patties instead of beef and includes a spicy mustard sauce. A McAloo Tikki (*aloo* is translated to "potato") is a patty of aloo with onion and tomato on a plain bun. The Paneer Salsa Wrap consists of a slab of
70 paneer (similar to cottage cheese) dredged in coating and fried, then added with a salad blend of lettuce, cabbage, and celery wrapped together with mayonnaise, salsa, and cheese. The Veg McCurry Pan is a rectangular, bowl-like crust filled with broccoli, baby corn, mushrooms, red bell
75 pepper, and a creamy sauce.

Variances in cultures can dictate an expansion model for any company venturing across borders. McDonald's regularly expands not only across America but also across the globe and must always have the best
80 interest of the customer in mind. For American world travelers, the trademarked golden *M*'s seen on a strange and busy foreign street may bring a sense of comfort and security, but the food served inside may, in fact, simply remind them of just how far from home they really are.

11. The third paragraph (lines 37-50) establishes all of the following EXCEPT that:

A.   different religions demand alternative food choices.
B.   McDonald's remains creative in its menu internationally.
C.   internationally, tastes vary greatly.
D.   McDonald's applies knowledge of Asian culture to its food offerings.

12. Which of the following statements about McDonald's is supported by the passage?

    F.   The restaurant chain always pleases its customers worldwide.
    G.   Customer demand dictates the food products McDonald's offers.
    H.   The restaurant chain's specialty items, such as the McRib, are highly sought after when they seasonally appear.
    J.   Stepping into a McDonald's overseas will force American customers to choose food other than what they are used to.

13. According to the passage, one of the few meat items available in an Indian McDonald's is the:

    A.   paneer.
    B.   Maharaja Mac.
    C.   Big Mac.
    D.   McAloo Tikki.

14. It can be reasonably inferred from the first paragraph that McDonald's recognizes Americans' increasing desire for:

    F.   additional condiments on traditional fare.
    G.   recognizable, classic McDonald's menu items.
    H.   more seafood options.
    J.   healthier menu choices.

15. The line "though not as peculiar to the American palate" (line 57) when referring to veggie burgers most likely demonstrates that:

    A.   veggie burgers have probably been consumed by Americans at some point in time.
    B.   there is at least one menu item that Americans will enjoy in any country overseas.
    C.   vegetables are eaten by Americans mainly in burger form, and if not, they are considered strange.
    D.   the vegetables in veggie burgers do not appeal to Americans.

16. It can reasonably be inferred that the intended audience for the passage is most likely:

    F.   Americans who are familiar with standard fast food offerings.
    G.   visitors to the U.S. from across the Atlantic Ocean.
    H.   American international travelers who desire a taste of home.
    J.   foodies who scour the world for innovative culinary creations.

17. According to the passage, a traveler in Québec could expect to find what kind of dish on McDonald's menu?

    A.   McRice.
    B.   Shogun Burger.
    C.   Poutine.
    D.   McCalabresa.

18. Which of the following statements best summarizes the second paragraph?

    F.   Americans of certain regions are quite obstinate about preserving their own culture's foods.
    G.   American McDonald's products are the most appetizing foods compared to those from around the globe.
    H.   Regional American items are not very different than standard American McDonald's menu items.
    J.   The regional tastes of Americans are a testament to McDonald's own roots.

19. What does the author mean by the statement, "but the food served inside may, in fact, simply remind them of just how far from home they really are" (lines 83-84)?

    A.   The iconic golden arches do not look like *M*'s in other countries.
    B.   Travelers who do not plan properly can be shocked by a different McDonald's menu.
    C.   Visiting a foreign McDonald's restaurant may be a sobering experience for a weary traveler.
    D.   Cultural differences amaze those who do not immerse themselves in that culture.

20. According to the passage, which of the following McDonald's menu items is NOT found in North America?

    F.   McWings
    G.   Green Chile Double Cheeseburger
    H.   Bratwurst
    J.   Cajun McChicken

Since its inception in 1981, MTV has long been dedicated to playing music videos, but over the last decade, the cable channel's focus has been retooled. Reality shows have become more and more prevalent on the station and actual "music television" has practically ceased to exist. Clearly MTV has lost touch with being a music television station—no longer should one expect music to be a major portion (or any part, for that matter) of its programming.

During the 1990s, MTV began rolling out programming that did not relate to its music television roots. *The Real World* (a reality show based on the interaction of strangers in a house) and *Road Rules* (a reality show based on the interaction of strangers in an RV) met with such great success that soon after, shows like *Singled Out* and *Loveline* infiltrated the home of music television. During the 2000s, reality shows truly began to permeate the fabric of MTV. By the time *Jackass, The Osbournes,* and *Laguna Beach* found large audiences, MTV had little choice but to make room for the reality juggernauts by removing more and more programs related to music. Initially a response to the influx of non-music television, 1998's *Total Request Live* (*TRL*), which aired weekdays and featured top videos, was pulled from the network in 2008 to accommodate more reality programming. This reduction in music television has hit its climax in that there are few music videos ever seen on MTV anymore.

MTV's continuing focus is on the reality genre. Recent titans such as *Teen Mom, True Life,* and *Catfish* have dominated the recent lineup and are well-known for their controversial topics or situations. Perhaps in efforts to appease those looking for the long lost "music television," (more likely to give credit to the artists), MTV has recently begun citing the artists and song names of the music being played on its reality shows. Whether through a small display on the bottom of the screen during the background song's duration or on its website, MTV has started offering viewers a chance to obtain the music heard on its station, just like in the early days when one would hear a song and purchase a record or cassette tape. Is this enough to satisfy viewers' cravings?

This technique of disguising the actual music seems to resemble, at least in part, MTV's controversial roots of devaluing the music played in favor of focusing on visual appeal. Critics of the early MTV stated that quality music was replaced with more visually pleasing acts—the focus from audio to visual was clear. Artists through the years have criticized MTV for this and insisted that the network uphold greater standards for their music videos. One music group in particular, The Dead Kennedys, released a song named "MTV, Get off the Air" in 1985 to criticize the station for their apparent practices. Maybe the network, in fact, did go off the air, choosing to move from music television to reality television.

Is MTV guilty of false advertising for moving to this new programming style? Wouldn't it be more accurate to change the name altogether from MTV to RTV (Reality Television)? In a possible attempt to be truer to its transformation, MTV dropped "Music Television" from its logo in 2010. Though seemingly a minor cosmetic alteration, this is a huge symbolic change for the network as well as for many of its viewers. Some MTV purists would certainly find this alteration to be a movement forever distancing MTV from its musical roots, while others may say, "It's about time." Other current loyal viewers may not even be aware of the change and are likely content with another thrilling episode of *Teen Mom.*

Certainly MTV has used viewer feedback and viewing data to transform what it once was and guide it into what it is now. With an ever-changing audience of older teens and twenty-somethings who grow out of MTV-style programs, there are new teens replacing them, finding new favorites. A teen viewer now may not even recognize that MTV once stood for "Music Television," thanks to the constant presence of reality shows. Where does this leave the network with the meaningless letters *M, T,* and *V*? Will generations in the future even know what MTV once stood for and how it got its start? As long as viewers keep tuning in, MTV executives will continue not to care.

21. The passage claims that MTV alters its programming largely based on:

    A.   how controversial the subject is.
    B.   avoiding everything that had already been done.
    C.   what can be considered "cutting edge."
    D.   viewing ratings.

22. According to the author, the most significant difference between *The Real World* and *Road Rules* is:

    F.   the challenges to accomplish.
    G.   the year each was launched.
    H.   the cast.
    J.   the setting.

23. The words *infiltrate* (line 16) and *permeate* (line 17) suggest the author feels reality shows have:

A. infested a station in which they do not belong.
B. hostilely taken over programming with little acceptance by the public.
C. infected the minds of the viewers.
D. allowed viewers to experience things they normally would not.

24. One of the main points the author seeks to make in the passage is that:

F. MTV's first audience is unsatisfied with its programming.
G. MTV should rethink its programming to match its acronym.
H. teens should be aware of MTV's roots.
J. MTV is careless with its programming.

25. The tone of this piece can best be described as:

A. ambiguous.
B. resentful.
C. refraining.
D. cruel.

26. Which of the following questions is NOT answered by information in the passage?

F. How long after its launch did it take MTV to begin showing reality shows?
G. What kind of programming would MTV purists like to see?
H. What time of night are videos actually aired on the network?
J. Why was *TRL* cancelled?

27. In the context of the passage, what does the author mean when he states, "This technique of disguising the actual music" (line 42)?

A. Contrasting music played in the past, today's songs shown on reality shows are readily available on the internet.
B. Compared to the early videos of MTV in which the music was secondary to the visual appeal, reality shows only use music as an accompaniment.
C. Contrasting modern music, songs written in previous decades are musically superior.
D. Compared to the music videos created in the '80s and '90s, modern videos pale in comparison visually.

28. In chronological order, the following events happened in what sequence?
    I. MTV removes "Music Television" from its logo.
    II. Critics claim that MTV was more concerned with videography than music quality.
    III. The Dead Kennedys release a song named "MTV Get Off The Air."

F. II, III, I
G. I, III, II
H. II, I, III
J. III, II, I

29. As it is used in line 32, the word *appease* can mean all of the following EXCEPT:

A. satisfy.
B. gratify.
C. pacify.
D. vilify.

30. The author of the article would likely agree with which of the following statements?

F. MTV should be off the air.
G. MTV values style over substance.
H. Audiences today only care about reality shows and not music.
J. Shows like *True Life* and *Teen Mom* promote unknown and indie artists.

Throughout history, many cultures have created legends of mysterious creatures; modern civilizations are no different. Bigfoot, the Loch Ness monster, the Jersey Devil, and werewolves have all incited fear not only in
5 children and adults alike, but also have spawned quests to find evidence of their existence. For years, one of these modern legends, the Chupacabra, has baffled cryptozoologists (researchers who study evidence or search for creatures whose reported existence is unproven). *Chupa-*
10 *cabra*, which literally means "goatsucker," is a mythological beast said to ravage regions in Puerto Rico, Brazil, and Mexico, as well as areas of the United States. The literal meaning of its name may be considered a misnomer, however, because it is said to attack all live-
15 stock and draining its blood. It reportedly leaves two puncture wounds in the neck of the animal but leaves the rest of the carcass intact. When mysterious deaths of livestock occur in these countries, speculation of the beast's existence is sure to follow.

20 Varying reports of the physiology of the Chupacabra often generate more questions than answers. Many who believe they saw the beast claim that it has red eyes; small, bat-like wings; and walks upright. Others look at the victim's wounds as evidence of two large protruding
25 fangs and knifelike claws. Still others liken the Chupacabra to a dog-like creature with longer hind legs and no hair. A multitude of videos and pictures exist pervasively on the internet enhancing the tale of both styles of Chupacabra, especially on YouTube where posters proudly tout
30 "*the* definitive piece of evidence" for the existence of the creature.

However, according to Benjamin Radford in an interview with ABC News reporter Ned Potter, the legend of the Chupacabra thrives on the imagination of the public
35 and intensifies by the first hand reports of those who claim to have seen one. Radford, author of the book, *Tracking the Chupacabra: The Vampire Beast in Fact, Fiction, and Folklore*, traced the origin of the myth to a Puerto Rican housewife named Madelyne Tolentino. To-
40 lentino recalled her 1995 experience (she shared it with the local news) to Radford for the interview: For only a matter of a minute or two, she saw a four foot tall creature standing on its hind legs with dark eyes, thin arms, and feathery spines on its back. There were only small holes
45 where its nose would be and three fingers on each paw. Naturally, UFO researchers picked up on the story. The tale spread on the internet and went viral.

During his interview, Radford acutely observed something interesting about Tolentino's story—it was
50 very detailed. In fact, it was too detailed for only a "minute or two" encounter. This was not the only suspicious detail to come out of the interview, though. Tolentino revealed to Radford that only weeks before the mysterious sighting, she had watched the movie *Species*. Radford
55 stated to ABC News, "To me, that was the smoking gun. It can't be a coincidence that this Chupacabra that's now popping up all over the world just happens to look exactly like the monster in this sci-fi film." Radford emphasizes that Tolentino was not intentionally lying or trying to cre-
60 ate a hoax. He believes that she was simply confused about what she saw, and her imagination ran wild. Radford shared his thoughts on the Chupacabra legend: "It doesn't matter what I write; it doesn't matter that I solved this. People are still going to see a weird hairless thing
65 and someone is going to call it a Chupacabra."

The report by Tolentino describes the upright walking creature that may have spawned the legend of the Chupacabra, but more recent reports tend to describe the hairless, dog-like creature as the mythical beast. A capture
70 in 2004 by a rancher near San Antonio, Texas, propagates the myth of the canine-esque being. He described a creature with strange jaw features and no hair. In this case, it was later determined by biologists to be a coyote of some sort with mange and facial deformities. Similar results
75 tend to emerge from other reports where the creatures were captured or found dead. Scientists generally deduce the beast is, in fact, some kind of canine creature with physical abnormalities, which may explain why people are reporting it as a Chupacabra. A creature like this is not
80 only a rare sight, but people generally fear the unknown and abnormal.

Although author Benjamin Radford claims to have solved the mystery of the Chupacabra, he shared his thoughts on why the creature continues to increase in no-
85 toriety with ABC News: "I think the bigger answer is that people like mysteries. And the idea of a beast that sucks goats' blood is kind of cool—it captures the public's imagination." Can one man's quest and subsequent book end the legend? At the current rate of growing popularity, one
90 can only predict that websites dedicated to the creature, reports of sightings, and evidence of the "real" Chupacabra will only increase in the future.

31. The main purpose of this passage is to:

    A. inform readers about the Chupacabra so that they can make an informed decision if they spot a creature that resembles what is described.
    B. present one researcher's findings in order to suggest that more research on the subject would be valuable.
    C. describe the biological makeup of the Chupacabra in order to compare it to common canines.
    D. discuss a mythological beast in order to illustrate how legends can grow from unusual circumstances and public interest.

32. The passage suggests all of the following as reasons for the legend's proliferation EXCEPT:

    F. the release of a book by Benjamin Radford.
    G. internet sensationalism.
    H. eye-witness accounts of the creature.
    J. news sources reporting on sightings.

33. The subtitle of Benjamin Radford's book refers to the Chupacabra as "*The Vampire Beast*" (line 37) due to the way the creature:

    A. leaves no trace of its existence.
    B. is nearly impossible to track.
    C. attacks its victims.
    D. is nocturnal.

34. It can be reasonably inferred that which of the following statements is true about why UFO researchers became involved in Tolentino's story?

    F. UFO researchers take an interest in any account of the unexplained.
    G. The local news reported her story as an alien encounter.
    H. UFO researchers are building a case that the Chupacabra is from another planet.
    J. The description by Tolentino resembles an alien from outer space.

35. The word *mange* in line 74 means:

    A. a skin disease resulting in hair loss.
    B. abnormal temperament and behavior.
    C. enlarged teeth.
    D. ability to walk on hind legs.

36. The author would most likely agree with which of the following statements?

    F. Mounting evidence of the Chupacabra, Bigfoot, and the Loch Ness monster prove that there are mysterious creatures roaming various parts of the Earth.
    G. Hunting legendary creatures can be an enjoyable past time.
    H. Legends like that of the Chupacabra exist due to public appeal and should only be used to entertain.
    J. Hoaxers who concoct stories about unidentified creatures are impeding researchers from unraveling the truth.

37. According to the passage, which of the following is NOT a reported physical feature of a Chupacabra?

    A. dark or red eyes
    B. membranous wings
    C. a protruding spinal column
    D. sharp claws

38. In the fourth paragraph, the sentence "To me, that was the smoking gun" (line 55) is an expression of the belief that:

    F. Tolentino watching *Species* was the catalyst for the creation of the hoax.
    G. Tolentino's earlier viewing of the film was conclusive evidence for her mistaken account of the creature.
    H. Tolentino could not properly see the beast due to a small smoke screen a gun might create.
    J. Tolentino still owns the weapon she used to shoot at the creature.

39. The author uses the description of YouTube posts about the Chupacabra (lines 29-31) in order to make all of the following points EXCEPT:

    A. a great amount of speculation exists about the Chupacabra.
    B. one cannot believe everything he or she sees.
    C. A YouTube user has posted a video featuring a real Chupacabra.
    D. websites can help spread legends.

40. It can be reasonably inferred from the passage that Benjamin Radford believes that:

    F. Tolentino created the entire story for fame and fortune.
    G. the monster from the sci-fi film *Species* was based on the Chupacabra.
    H. the Chupacabra exists, but is a hairless, canine-type creature and not the kind described by Tolentino.
    J. reports of sightings are attributed to confusion and imagination.

Test 2

ENGLISH

75 questions

45 minutes

ANSWER SHEET-ENGLISH TEST 2

1._____	16._____	31._____	46._____	61._____
2._____	17._____	32._____	47._____	62._____
3._____	18._____	33._____	48._____	63._____
4._____	19._____	34._____	49._____	64._____
5._____	20._____	35._____	50._____	65._____
6._____	21._____	36._____	51._____	66._____
7._____	22._____	37._____	52._____	67._____
8._____	23._____	38._____	53._____	68._____
9._____	24._____	39._____	54._____	69._____
10._____	25._____	40._____	55._____	70._____
11._____	26._____	41._____	56._____	71._____
12._____	27._____	42._____	57._____	72._____
13._____	28._____	43._____	58._____	73._____
14._____	29._____	44._____	59._____	74._____
15._____	30._____	45._____	60._____	75._____

500 Million Friends

Imagine having 500 million friends. A few years ago, such a notion would have sounded absurd, but with Facebook, making connections **(1)have never been** easier.

(2)Rumor has it, Facebook started as a way to meet **(3)girls (or at least to look at pictures of girls)**. Soon, **(4)they** became an internet sensation.

(5)In just a few short years, Mark Zuckerberg went from living in a college dorm room to becoming an accidental billionaire.

Zuckerberg was not motivated by wealth, however. In fact, when he was only in high school, **(6)Zuckerberg could have made a lot of money by selling a music program to Microsoft**; he turned them down. It is doubtful that Zuckerberg anticipated **Facemash(7)** to eventually bring him billions of dollars;

1. A. NO CHANGE
   B. has never been
   C. had never been
   D. never has been

2. Should the writer DELETE the underlined portion?
   F. YES, because this article is based on facts, not rumor.
   G. YES, because it undermines the author's credibility.
   H. NO, because the site's true origins are not important.
   J. NO, because this statement has not been confirmed.

3. All of the following changes are acceptable EXCEPT:
   A. girls, or at least to look at pictures of girls
   B. girls. Or at least to look at pictures of girls
   C. girls–or at least to look at pictures of girls
   D. girls

4. F. NO CHANGE
   G. it
   H. he
   J. those

5. The underlined portion can NOT be placed:
   A. where it is now.
   B. after *Zuckerberg* (lowercasing *in*).
   C. after *billionaire* (lowercasing *in*).
   D. after *living* (lowercasing *in*).

6. Which of the following expressions would best maintain the tone and style of the passage?
   F. NO CHANGE
   G. Zuckerberg had a chance to make bank through a deal with Microsoft.
   H. Microsoft made him a lucrative offer to purchase a music program he created.
   J. Zuckerberg was an idiot when Microsoft offered him a once-in-a-lifetime deal.

7. Suppose the writer were considering adding the following phrase: *, the precursor to Facebook,* after *Facemash*. Should the writer make this change?

   A. YES, because it explains the term Facemash.
   B. YES, because it reminds readers that this article is about Facebook, not Facemash.
   C. No, because the addition would make the sentence grammatically incorrect.
   D. No, because everyone knows that Facemash is the earlier name for what later became Facebook.

(8)according to legend, he and his friends just wanted to look at pictures of girls. After just a few days of launching Facemash, a site in which viewers could rank fellow students' attractiveness, Harvard shut the site down **(9)in spite of** an overwhelming increase in internet traffic.

Shortly thereafter, Zuckerberg wrote the program for Facebook **(10)(originally referred to as The Facebook)**, a portal for Harvard students to connect with one another. While it first was limited to Harvard, the popularity of the site led **(11)it to slowly be expanded** to other schools, **(12)mostly** on the East Coast. Word of mouth spread until schools across the nation were requesting access to the site; the exclusivity was part of the allure.

Not everyone was thrilled about the up-and-coming site, however. In particular, two of Zuckerberg's **(13)classmates twins Cameron and Tyler Winklevoss,** accused Zuckerberg of stealing their idea, claiming they had first sought out Zuckerberg's help in developing their concept of Harvard Connect, a site with a similar concept. After years of litigation, the parties settled for

8. Which of the following substitutions for the underlined portion would be LEAST appropriate?
   F. allegedly,
   G. supposedly,
   H. without a doubt,
   J. some say

9. A. NO CHANGE
   B. due to
   C. to put a stop to
   D. , because of

10. Should the writer delete the underlined portion?
    F. YES, because it is an unnecessary detail.
    G. YES, because there is not a big difference between Facebook and The Facebook.
    H. NO, because there is a big difference between Facebook and The Facebook.
    J. NO, because it shows how Facebook has changed over time.

11. A. NO CHANGE
    B. him to slowly expand it
    C. Zuckerberg to slowly expand the site
    D. to slow expansion

12. All of the following substitutions for the underlined portion are acceptable EXCEPT:

    F. primarily
    G. especially
    H. exclusively
    J. mainly

13. A. NO CHANGE
    B. classmates; twins Camerson and Tyler Winklevoss
    C. classmates: twins Cameron and Tyler Winklevoss
    D. classmates, twins Cameron and Tyler Winklevoss,

an undisclosed sum (though some estimates put it in the $20 million range).

Now that Facebook is such a normal part of everyday life, **(14)it's hard to believe** that such an influential social media tool was the result of the boredom and innovation of a college student. Perhaps Zuckerberg's modesty is one of the main contributors to his success; instead of looking for a way to make money, he followed his passion, and through his **(15)intelligence, dedication, and the fact that he was good at computer programming**, an astronomical fortune just happened to be a bonus.

14. F. NO CHANGE
    G. its hard to believe
    H. its crazy to think
    J. who would of thought

15. A. NO CHANGE
    B. genius, devotion, and interest in computer programming,
    C. ability to be dedicated, good at, and smart about computer programming,
    D. brain, relentless hours programming, and his knack for it,

Freegans

Everyone loves free stuff, but for freegans, freebies are not just a bonus, **(16)its** a way of life. Freegans believe in limiting the amount of resources humans consume. **(17)Hating to see food, clothes, and other resources go to waste. Freegans** aim to reuse goods that others are quick to throw away.

A visit to one of New York City's Garbage Tours **(18)reveals** just how much people waste. Freegans **(19)looking** through dumpsters behind stores and restaurants to salvage food and possessions. Often times, they leave with bags full of food, enough to provide a week or two worth of groceries. **(20)While** many people find this practice disgusting, it is not as bad as it sounds. The freegans do not eat old, rotten, moldy food; **(21)rather,** they often find fresh produce along with packaged goods, **(22)even milk,** is not yet past its expiration date. In a world where many

16. F. NO CHANGE
    G. it's
    H. their
    J. they're

17. A. NO CHANGE
    B. Hating to see food, clothes, and other resources go to waste, freegans
    C. Freegans hate to see food, clothes, and other resources go to waste and they
    D. Hating to see food, clothes, and other resources go to waste;

18. F. NO CHANGE
    G. show
    H. highlight
    J. demonstrate

19. A. NO CHANGE
    B. have searched
    C. rummage
    D. will canvass

20. All of the following alternatives to the underlined portion are acceptable EXCEPT:
    F. Although
    G. Even though
    H. Despite the fact that
    J. Yet

21. Which of the following transitional words or expressions would be the LEAST appropriate replacement for the underlined portion?
    A. meanwhile,
    B. instead,
    C. as a matter of fact,
    D. in fact,

22. F. NO CHANGE
    G. even milk, though
    H. even milk that
    J. even milk which

people go to bed hungry, **(23)it is startling and alarming** to see how much good food is wasted.

[1] Many freegans also furnish their homes and clothe themselves with used goods, finding things like clothing, dishes, **(24) and even** furniture and appliances in good working condition. [2]Although freegans manage to save a lot of money, their motivation is not frugality. [3]Freegans are often **(25)environmentalists; realizing** the impact that overconsumption has on the environment, from waste filling landfills to the resources **(26) and energy required** to produce goods. [4]Additionally, many freegans wish to free themselves from the materialistic lives of many Americans. [5]By focusing less on possessions, freegans have more time to devote to other interests, often allowing them to pursue less profitable, yet more fulfilling, jobs. **[27]**

[1]Many people may not be inclined to dig through a dumpster, but **(28)perhaps** shopping at a resale shop would be a good start. [2]While freeganism may seem extreme, it is easy to reduce waste on a smaller scale. [3]Instead of finding food in a garbage can, go to the local grocery store or bakery and ask for day old bread or other items before **(29)they get dumped**. [4]There are also websites that allow people to connect and share free items with one another, thus giving new life to the expression, "One man's trash is another man's treasure." **[30]**

23.
A. NO CHANGE
B. strangely unusual
C. shocking
D. unfortunate and sad

24.
F. NO CHANGE
G. including
H. such as
J. like

25.
A. NO CHANGE
B. environmentalists who realizes
C. environmentalists whom realize
D. environmentalists who realize

26.
F. NO CHANGE
G. and materials
H. and supplies
J. and equipment

27. Which sentence expresses the main idea of this paragraph?
A. Sentence 1
B. Sentence 2
C. Sentence 4
D. Sentence 5

28. The writer is considering deleting the underlined portion. Should this change be made?

F. YES, because it sounds uncertain.
G. YES, because it is unnecessary.
H. NO, because it conveys a gentle suggestion.
J. NO, because it provides concrete directions for the reader.

29.
A. NO CHANGE
B. it's trashed.
C. it gets tossed.
D. they are discarded.

30. The most logical order for the sentences in this paragraph is:

F. 1, 2, 3, 4
G. 2, 1, 3, 4
H. 1, 2, 4, 3
J. 4, 2, 3, 1

Crazy College Classes

[1]

Many people believe that the college experience is pretty **(31)typical; study**, pull the occasional all-nighter, and maybe even party a bit. **(32)Because** students major in different subjects, they tend to take similar general education courses, such as rhetoric, psychology, or economics. What many prospective students **(33)may not realize. However, is that** college classes can be unlike anything they have ever experienced before. **[34]**

[2]

Take literature classes, for instance. **(35)In addition to studying** the traditional canon of Shakespeare, Dickens, and Homer, students have the option **(36)of reading about** zombies, hobbits, and even *The Simpsons.* The University of Wisconsin offers a course in Elvish language from *The Lord of the Rings,*

31. A. NO CHANGE
     B. typical: Study,
     C. typical, study,
     D. typical—study,

32. F. NO CHANGE
     G. However, because
     H. Although
     J. Since

33. A. NO CHANGE
     B. may not realize, however is that
     C. may not realize; however,
     D. may not realize, however, is that

34. Which of the following statements, taking into consideration the content and style of the passage, would be the most appropriate ending for the paragraph?
     F. In fact, school can be—dare we say—fun!
     G. It's time to buckle down and study hard.
     H. Many students have a difficult time making the transition from high school to college.
     J. Subjects like rhetoric, psychology, and economics are not offered in some high schools.

35. A. NO CHANGE
     B. In addition, students study
     C. In addition to study
     D. In addition, to study

36. F. NO CHANGE
     G. to read of
     H. for reading about
     J. to read about

(37)while Columbia College Chicago offers *The Simpsons* as Satirical Authors (The University of California at Berkley**(38), meanwhile,** situates the

The Simpsons in its philosophy department). **(39)And** while the *Twilight* series may not have received top marks from renowned literary critics, that isn't stopping the University of Alabama from offering a special literature class devoted to the franchise.

[3]

Fans of video games don't have to skip class to play all day. **(40)In fact,** enroll in Oberlin College's physical education class—students learn virtual combat techniques via the Nintendo Game Cube. Meanwhile, at UNC Greensboro, professors use an alien-themed video game that incorporates the curriculum and even the homework.

[4]

Perhaps the most unusual course offering is out of UC Santa Clara, where students have the option of studying The Joy of Garbage. What may sound like a joke is **(41)totally** a serious learning experience in which

37. Which of the following options is LEAST acceptable?
    A. whereas
    B. and
    C. as
    D. while

38. The underlined portion could be replaced with all of the following EXCEPT:
    F. , in the meantime,
    G. , similarly,
    H. , on the other hand,
    J. , conversely,

39. Is it appropriate to begin this sentence with the word *And*?
    A. YES, because it introduces an additional example.
    B. YES, because it builds upon the previous point and fits with the passage's informal tone.
    C. NO, because it creates a sentence fragment.
    D. NO, because the preceding and following sentences should be combined.

40.　　F. NO CHANGE
　　　G. Instead,
　　　H. Rather,
　　　J. You should

41.　　A. NO CHANGE
　　　B. as a matter of fact
　　　C. seriously
　　　D. actually

students explore issues like **(42)waste, decomposing, and sanitation issues**. Students even take field trips to landfills and sewage facilities.

[5]

Some people are critical of these creative course offerings, **(43)and they argue** that they make a joke out of institutions of higher education. Other opponents argue that the classes are little more than a money-making **(44) scheme, luring students** away from partaking in more educational classes. Many students, though, love the options, and find them not just fun, but as genuine, interesting learning experiences as well.

[45]

42.   F. NO CHANGE
      G. waste, decomposition, and sanitation issues.
      H. waste, decomposing, and sanitizing.
      J. waste, decomposition, and sanitation.

43.   A. NO CHANGE
      B. making the argument
      C. arguing
      D. with the argument

44. All of the following substitutions for the underlined portion are acceptable EXCEPT:
      F. scheme that lures students
      G. scheme, which lures students
      H. scheme to lure students
      J. scheme for students lured

45. Suppose the writer wanted to add in the following detail:

   Students at NYU learn music through the game Guitar Hero in the class Music, Video Games, and the Nature of Human Cognition.

The sentence should be placed at the end of paragraph:
      A. 2
      B. 3
      C. 4
      D. 5

Will You Go to Prom with Me?

The flurry of activity that surrounds prom season usually focuses on the girls, who have to find the perfect dress and killer shoes while trying to coordinate with their dates and plan the perfect night. However, in recent years boys have taken on an extra **(46) job and responsibility** known as the "prom proposal." Now, asking a girl to prom is almost as monumental an event as the dance itself.

(47)Increasingly, prom proposals' popularity in the past decade, fueled by the former MTV show *Laguna Beach*, in which male students went to great lengths (even donning gorilla suits) to catch the attention of their **(48)potential** prom dates. These proposals often feed into males' competitiveness **(49)with boys trying** to outdo one another with crazy, outlandish, and either romantic or humorous ideas.

The proposals are becoming increasingly public as well. In many cases, the whole school

46.   F. NO CHANGE
      G. requirement
      H. task
      J. obstacle

47.   A. NO CHANGE
      B. Having increased, prom proposals are more popular
      C. More popular are prom proposals, which have increased
      D. Prom proposals have increased in popularity

48. All of the following are acceptable EXCEPT:
      F. possible
      G. perpetual
      H. prospective
      J. probable

49. Which of the following would NOT be acceptable?
      A. as boys try
      B. with boys vying
      C. for boys will try
      D. while boys can try

(50)watches and waits to hear how the girl will answer the prospective date's plea. Young men have **(51)taken to placing** announcements over the school intercom, on scoreboards, or even on the internet. Girls have been surprised by a serenade during class, decorations on their cars, and even pizzas with toppings spelling out "PROM?" **[52]**

One Connecticut student's creative idea landed him in hot water. **(53)Him and his friends** adhered giant cardboard letters to the entrance of their **(54) high school, to greet** students as they arrived for class the next morning. **(55)The girl said** "yes," school administrators were not as thrilled. The **(56)student along with his friends who helped him was** suspended, and since school policy dictated that any student suspended after April 1st could not attend prom, he and his friends were banned from the dance as well.

50.   F. NO CHANGE
      G. witnesses
      H. will be a part of
      J. anticipate and wait for

51.   A. NO CHANGE
      B. been inclined to place
      C. decided to make
      D. made

52. Which of the following options would be the best conclusion for this paragraph?
      F. Some girls are embarrassed by these spectacles.
      G. Whatever the method, the idea seems to be, "The bigger the better."
      H. Some of these ideas sound really stupid.
      J. A shy boy may not want to do this.

53.   A. NO CHANGE
      B. His friends and him
      C. He and his friends
      D. They

54.   F. NO CHANGE
      G. high school to greet
      H. high school which greeted
      J. high school, and they greeted

55.   A. NO CHANGE
      B. Because the girl said
      C. However, the girl said,
      D. While the girl said

56.   F. NO CHANGE
      G. student, along with his friends who helped him, were
      H. student, along with his friends who helped him, was
      J. student—along with his friends who helped him— were

Many people thought the punishment was extreme for a young man **(57)with good intentions and he said** he was just trying to be creative and romantic.

38,000 people supported a Facebook petition **(58)urging** the school to lessen the punishment, and the story even made national news. **(59)Soon, over time,** he and his date were allowed to attend prom. [60]

57.   A. NO CHANGE
      B. with good intentions, and they said
      C. with good intentions who later said
      D. OMIT the underlined portion.

58. Which of the following choices is NOT acceptable?
      F. to urge
      G. encouraging
      H. for urging
      J. that encouraged

59.   A. NO CHANGE
      B. Additionally,
      C. Eventually,
      D. OMIT the underlined portion

60. Which of the following statements would be the best conclusion for this passage?

      F. This was one prom proposal that turned out to be even more memorable than intended.
      G. A great way to propose to a prom date, then, is to get your story on the news.
      H. Principals obviously can't take a joke.
      J. The best prom proposals are daring and controversial.

The Real Dracula

With the popularity of television shows like *The Vampire Diaries* and *True Blood,* along with the **(61)infamous and notorious** *Twilight* **(62)film series and books** vampires are a huge pop culture success. **(63)Obviously,** these fantastic creatures are a work of pure fiction. However, many **(64) Twi-hards** may be surprised to learn that the most well-known vampire of **(65)all the one and only Dracula** has his roots in true history.

(66)Author Bram Stoker based the title character of his 1897 novel *Dracula* on Vlad III, Prince of Wallachia, Transylvania **(67)(now Romania).** The name Dracula means **(68)"Son of the Dragon" and** his father was often referred to as Vlad the Dragon, a sign of

61.   A. NO CHANGE
      B. well-known and popular
      C. popular
      D. notorious and well-known

62.   F. NO CHANGE
      G. film, series, and books
      H. film series, and books,
      J. film series and books,

63.   A. NO CHANGE
      B. Surprisingly,
      C. Interestingly,
      D. Importantly,

64.   F. NO CHANGE
      G. genre's fans
      H. fans of the genre
      J. OMIT the underlined portion

65.   A. NO CHANGE
      B. all, the one and only Dracula,
      C. all: the one and only Dracula
      D. all; the one and only Dracula

66. All of the following choices are acceptable EXCEPT:
      F. Author, Bram Stoker,
      G. Bram Stoker
      H. Bram Stoker, a famous author,
      J. The author Bram Stoker

67. Should the author of the passage delete the underlined portion?
      A. YES, because it is irrelevant to the subject of the passage.
      B. YES, because the passage is about the past, not the present.
      C. NO, because it provides relevant information that is referenced later in the passage.
      D. NO, because it provides an interesting geography fact.

68.   F. NO CHANGE
      G. "Son of the Dragon", and
      H. "Son of the Dragon;" and
      J. "Son of the Dragon," and

his membership in the Order of the Dragon. The group

(69)was committed to fending off invading Ottoman

Turks. Both father and son were characterized by their

cruel mid-15th century reign, with their names taking on

new meaning in the modern day, as *dracul* means

"devil" in **(70) contemporary current** Romania.

Vlad III lived up to his reputation. Estimates

have him responsible for the deaths of **(71)anywhere**

from: 40,000 to 80,000 people, not including residents

of the many villages he ordered burned to the ground.

He also favored using extremely **(72)violent and cruel**

methods of torture on his **(73)victims in his ruthless**

quest for power. On several occasions, he invited guests

to dine with him, only to imprison, torture, or murder

them after the meal.

Vlad III's legacy began to be immortalized in

German and Russian literature, with accounts of his

reign of terror being recorded in short stories. These

69. The underlined portion could be replaced with all of the following EXCEPT:
    A. committed to
    B. had a commitment to
    C. committing to
    D. made a commitment to

70.   F. NO CHANGE
    G. contemporary, current
    H. present-day
    J. OMIT the underlined portion

71.   A. NO CHANGE
    B. a huge range of,
    C. numbers that vary from:
    D. anywhere from

72. Which of the following changes is the LEAST acceptable?
    F. malicious techniques
    G. agonizing means
    H. irate approaches
    J. brutal modes

73.   A. NO CHANGE
    B. victims, in his ruthless
    C. victims; in his ruthless
    D. victims. In his ruthless

anthologies referred to the prince as **(74)Dracula. Thus** cementing his nickname in literature. In his research of Romanian history in the 1800s, Stoker came across the name Dracula and found it fitting for the villain of his novel. While modern readers equate the name Dracula with a blood-thirsty monster, many historical accounts portray the real Dracula in a somewhat positive light, regarding him as a heroic warrior who valiantly defended his nation against invaders. [75]

74.   F. NO CHANGE
       G. Dracula, thus
       H. Dracula; thus
       J. Dracula: thus,

75. Suppose the writer aimed to explain the recent popularity of vampires amongst teenagers. Would this passage fulfill that purpose?

   A. YES, because it mentions hit shows and movies like *True Blood* and *Twilight*.

   B. YES, because it explains how earlier vampire stories influenced modern-day writers.

   C. NO, because it focuses on the historical figure behind a famous literary vampire.

   D. NO, because much of the article is about Romania, not America.

END OF ENGLISH TEST 2

Test 2

READING

40 questions

35 minutes

ANSWER SHEET- READING TEST 2

1.____   11.____   21.____   31.____

2.____   12.____   22.____   32.____

3.____   13.____   23.____   33.____

4.____   14.____   24.____   34.____

5.____   15.____   25.____   35.____

6.____   16.____   26.____   36.____

7.____   17.____   27.____   37.____

8.____   18.____   28.____   38.____

9.____   19.____   29.____   39.____

10.____   20.____   30.____   40.____

PASSAGE I—PROSE FICTION   "Resurrection Mary"

"Come on, Jerry. You know we love hearing your story!" an older man holding a mug pleaded from a few barstools down. "Besides, it's almost Halloween and I haven't had a good fright in years!"

5   "Gentlemen," Jerry responded to the small but attentive group of men, "why is it you always want to hear the story so late at night? I'm tired and need to get some shut eye," Jerry responded with a grin and a twinkle in his eye.

10   All eyes remained on Jerry, occasionally lured away by the temptation of the beverages sitting in front of the customers. "One's on me if you get started," urged the man next to Jerry.

      Jerry sighed and placed his order with the bar-
15   tender through a curl of his fingers. "Now, you all recall I was just a young buck, back in 1939. Woo-wee, could I cut a rug! Anyhow, I was down on 47th Street at the dance hall that used to be there and I saw this very pretty girl down there a few times, always just standing by the
20   wall. I never did see her with any guy, but me being me, never mustered up the guts to ask her to dance. Well, I finally asked her to dance with me this one night and that's when everything changed."

      Jerry had the full attention of the bar after his
25   first few words. The bartender handled Jerry's order by touch alone, never breaking focus on the storyteller. "So I ask her to dance," Jerry continued. "We spent the rest of the night dancing together. She was just the prettiest little thing in her white dress, but I have to say that she
30   seemed a little distant or something. Like when you have something on your mind, you know?" Jerry addressed his audience, but they all knew the question was just rhetorical. "I think things are going well enough to steal a little smooch from her, so I do. It turns out her lips are
35   as cold as a wet fish."

      A barfly shouted, "Jerry has never been able to warm up the ladies!" immediately followed by a hoarse laugh and a slap of the countertop. This breaks the stupors of the audience. Some laugh, others shoot warnings.

40   "You're wrong on that one, Joe!" Jerry lightly defended. The laughter died moments after Jerry's next words. "And that's when I noticed I had been holding hands with this girl dancing the whole time and her hands are freezing, too. Naturally, I don't think much of
45   it because right after that little peck, she asks me to take her home." Jerry fought off a smirk and continued. "She tells me to take Archer Avenue back to her place, but

Archer Avenue is far out of the way. I know because she told me where about she lived earlier on. I try to tell her
50   that, but she just said it again, really slow and sort of focused or something: 'I want to go down Archer.' Being the gentleman that I am, though, I respect the lady's wishes and head down Archer." Jerry unconsciously wiped his glass.

55   "So we're driving and all the while she's just staring out the window. Really kind of freaky, you know?" The crowd gives no response again. "And you all know down Archer there is Resurrection Cemetery. So we're driving right by it and she tells me, 'I need to
60   get out here.' I'm thinking finally this girl shows a little life by joking around! I chuckle but keep driving. She tells me again. I look over and she's just still staring like a zombie out that window. I start to pull over and begin wondering what I did wrong for a pretty thing to want to
65   get out next to a cemetery in the middle of the night. 'Okay,' I say, 'but I'm walking with you to wherever it is you're going. I'm not letting you walk around out here alone.' Now guys, this is the part that really made my heart pound. In a slow, soft voice, she said, 'This is
70   where I have to get out, but you can't follow me to where I'm going.'"

      Jerry took a swig and the rest of the audience followed his lead. "So I start to turn to her to say something because at this point I'm really confused. Before I
75   could say anything, she opens the door and takes off to the cemetery gates. I'm watching her and her white dress, and all of a sudden, right before my very own eyes, and I swear this on my dear old mama's grave, she up and vanishes before she reaches the gates." Jerry
80   tensely rubbed his glass. "I must have turned whiter than her dress. She was a danged apparition! I was dancing with a specter! I held hands with and even kissed a ghost!"

      The air was still. Jaws hung open, eyes dried
85   out. Jerry was the only one who moved, and that was to slide off his barstool. "I don't really remember the rest of that night aside from getting the heck out of there! I thought about it constantly, though, and a while later I go down and visit the address she had told me about when
90   we were dancing. I knocked on the door and this woman answered. I tell her about everything, and she just kept on shaking her head saying, 'No, that can't be.' She said her daughter, who did match my description, I might add, had been dead for several years. She was buried in a
95   flowing white dress at Resurrection Cemetery. She even showed me a picture of the family, and, I swear on my

48

dear old mama's grave, that was the girl in the picture. No doubt in my mind. I was totally shocked, you know? It was the kind of shock where you can't think of any-
100 thing else except the incident. And that is certainly what I did, and still do, and especially when you all don't let me get home!" Jerry mocked frustration. The crowd broke out of their mesmeric trance. Drinks were guzzled and lungs were filled.

105   "Take it easy, gentlemen. It's time to hit the hay," Jerry announced. The audience responded with their own farewells.

One called out to Jerry as he walked toward the door, "Hey, did you even catch her name? Did her mom
110 agree with the name you gave her?"

"I can't remember her name for certain," Jerry replied, "but now she's just sort of a new person, you know? She kind of lives on in the story, and through the story, her name has become Resurrection Mary."

115

1. The narrator likely smirks (line 46) because:

   A. he knows his way around the neighborhood and knows that her directions are incorrect.
   B. he is telling an elaborate lie to his audience and is getting away with it.
   C. he knew that after the kiss, there was no connection between the two and wished to end the night.
   D. he is bragging to his audience about how the girl wanted to spend time with him alone.

2. The main point of the first three paragraphs is to:

   F. demonstrate how Jerry is easily persuaded.
   G. acclimate the reader to the setting.
   H. emphasize the customers' fixations on their beverages.
   J. elaborate on the general stereotype that stories are shared at taverns.

3. It can be reasonably inferred from the passage that the narrator would best be described as which of the following in interactions with women?

   A. Courteous and respectful.
   B. Masculine and boastful.
   C. Forward and persuasive.
   D. Withdrawn and elusive.

4. The statement "Drinks were guzzled and lungs were filled" (lines 103-104) functions in the passage to support which of the following?

   F. The customers have only two basic needs.
   G. The audience takes a short break from the shock of the tale.
   H. The tale is entirely too long for this audience.
   J. The customers break their intense focus and return to normal behavior.

5. It can be reasonably inferred that the term "shoot warnings" (line 39) refers to the:

   A. additional clever statements influenced by the first joke.
   B. firing of handguns in response to a witty comment.
   C. non-verbal message that some customers are not amused by the interrupting quip.
   D. vocalized reactions that the joking individual has had enough to drink for the night.

6. The narrator and his audience's attitudes toward each other are most likely ones of:

   F. rapid evasiveness.
   G. open antagonism.
   H. mutual respect.
   J. calming relief.

7. The author repeatedly uses vernacular phrases like "you know?" and "I swear on my dear old mama's grave" in order to:

   A. remind the reader discreetly of the familiarity of death.
   B. develop the understanding through language that the story is being told causally and among friends.
   C. aid the reader in understanding the intellectual level of the narrator, and, therefore, the validity of the story.
   D. speak directly to the reader to create a bond with the narrator.

8. All of the following are details Jerry provides about the about the apparition EXCEPT:

   F. a glowing white dress.
   G. icy lips.
   H. chilled fingers.
   J. her disappearance near the cemetery.

9. Which of the following is NOT evidence to support the fact that many of the customers have heard Jerry's story before?

    A.   The promptness in which the customers focus on Jerry's story.
    B.   The offer to buy Jerry a drink if he tells the tale.
    C.   Jerry providing background information in the story about himself as a young man.
    D.   A man pleading with Jerry to tell the story.

10. It can be reasonably inferred that Jerry is still nervous when telling the story because of his:

    F.   rubbing of his glass.
    G.   sudden eagerness to leave.
    H.   colloquial phrasing.
    J.   grin and twinkle in his eye.

BLANK PAGE PROVIDED

TURN TO THE NEXT PASSAGE

Sign language has long been known to be a variation of communication that utilizes hands as a replacement for a voice. Used mainly through necessity, signing takes longer than speaking and requires education
5 and practice to implement effectively. However, through technology, the world is becoming more accustomed to and reliant upon a new kind of communication spoken through the hands. This new method is fast becoming the preferred means of communication among friends, and it
10 can be done across town or across the world. Signed words, and even spoken syllables, should move aside for the digital characters appearing on nearly every cell phone—the text message brings a new meaning to communicating with the hands, even if it's all thumbs.

15 Short message service (SMS), often referred to as texting, is a modern technology that allows a message to be sent from one cell phone to another or through the web to a cell phone. First developed in the early 1980s for sending service notification to customers of mobile
20 phones from the service provider, the technology was truly defined in 1992 when European engineer Neil Papworth of Sema Group sent the first person-to-person message via the Vodafone network from a computer to the mobile phone of Richard Jarvis. "Merry Christmas,"
25 Papworth texted, but this technology was not attractively gift-wrapped in a shiny little bow just yet—companies had to set up systems to properly charge their customers for the service. It would take a few years, but telecommunication companies soon reaped the benefits of cleverly
30 priced messaging plans that can leave even the most frugal cell phone user shocked with the bill.

How many teens have incurred an astronomical phone bill thanks to the combination of hundreds, if not thousands, of texts and a limiting plan? Perhaps you per-
35 sonally have incurred the wrath of an irate parent who must make up hundreds of dollars to pay an overage. Cell phone companies such as Verizon and AT&T are making it easier to avoid these "life-threatening" moments with unlimited texting bundles, but these may end up costing a
40 bundle. Data plans with free texts may save money in the long run, allowing teens to freely text until their thumbs go numb, but these can be costly. Plans that cost money per text still exist; however, many have learned the hard way that pay per text can challenge the restraint of the
45 most avid texters.

16,000. That's the number of texts sent by teen Kate Moore, 2009 US national texting champion, in one month. For those not interested in doing the math, that averages to approximately 533 texts a day. That equates
50 to over twenty-two texts an hour, and that's not even accounting for everyday activities, like eating, bathing, and sleeping. A good night's sleep may be an overlooked necessity for many teens that yield to the urge of constant social attentiveness.

55 Recent studies assayed the impact frequent messaging can have on a teen. Sleep deprivation and anxiety are becoming regular afflictions for those who leave their phones on during the night to send and receive texts from friends, which certainly affects the daily activities that
60 demand attention and concentration. Additionally, many run the risk of automobile accidents due to the desire to text and read messages while driving. This has prompted nearly every U.S. state to adopt laws prohibiting the use of cell phones while operating motor vehicles. To approx-
65 imately 63% of teens who admitted in a 2011 survey that they text while driving, staying in the social loop apparently trumps the law and the risk of serious injury or death. It is quite clear that our phones are greatly interfering with our health and safety.

70 This relatively new form of communication doesn't always bring with it potential harm. Instead of fretting about high phone bills and sleepless nights, some talented texters hone their skills and compete in texting contests. In 2010, the first LG Mobile World Cup in
75 Manhattan pitted teams of two against other teams from thirteen countries across the globe, all vying for the first place prize of $100,000. The pairs competed in a five round challenge taxing thumbs, reactions, and nerves. The winning team, Team Korea, won the competition by tex-
80 ting 120 words in 2 minutes, 26 seconds, while Team USA finished second by completing the short paragraph 22 seconds later. Also showcased at the event was Pedro Matias of Portugal, who set a new Guinness World Record for texting by typing a 264-character message on a
85 smartphone in under two minutes (1:59 to be exact), annihilating the old record by twenty-three seconds. Contestants of all events could not abbreviate or have any typos and typed the same number of characters as their competitors in their own native language.

90 Humanity continues to excel in creating new manners of expressing oneself in areas that once left gaps. We have learned to communicate with our hands for those who cannot hear, with our voices to those across town, and with our keystrokes to those across the world. New
95 technology enables the ordinary person to communicate with others across the globe and be introduced to other cultures and people—it is just another way technology has put the world at our fingertips.

11. It can reasonably be inferred from the passage that the author would agree with which of the following statements?

A. Advancing technology will likely be the cause of a great disconnect among humanity.
B. New technology should never replace the old methods of communication.
C. Other countries like South Korea are better with new technology than the United States.
D. New technology can alter our everyday lives.

12. Which of the following most accurately states the main idea of the sixth paragraph (lines 70-89)?

F. Fame and fortune lie in wait for any who text with speed and accuracy.
G. The contest proves that texting can be more than just a means of communication.
H. Texting allows for people of all countries to come together, much like the sports of the Olympic Games.
J. New technology always brings with it exciting new contests that gauge its users' abilities.

13. It can be reasonably inferred from the passage that the author believes that sign language is:

A. uncomplicated.
B. cryptic.
C. maddening.
D. antiquated.

14. Which of the following claims is NOT supported by the passage?

F. Long distance communication is responsible for a decreasing amount of face-to-face dialogue.
G. Texting can be a danger for those who use it irresponsibly.
H. Choosing the right phone contract to accommodate for texting can be financially smart.
J. Texting technology was originally created to send information from a company to an individual.

15. The author uses the term "life-threatening" (line 38) in order to:

A. emphasize the fear teens may have if they go over their text allowance.
B. caution those who text more than their plan allows.
C. threaten teens into submission to their parents.
D. diffuse a highly-charged topic with an extreme result.

16. According to the passage, who or what is most directly responsible for developing text messaging as it is known today?

F. Richard Jarvis.
G. Vodafone.
H. Neil Papworth.
J. Kate Moore.

17. In the fifth paragraph, the phrase "Sleep deprivation and anxiety are becoming regular afflictions" (lines 56-57), is an expression of the belief that:

A. texting is the cause of a surge in teen hospital visits.
B. teens are so scared about missing a text that sleep becomes unimportant.
C. teens' lives are adversely affected by the increased social involvement created by texting.
D. phone companies should establish parental locks on phones dictating when a teen can use a phone.

18. By including the average daily texts sent by teenager Kate Moore, the author implies:

F. all teenagers have addictions to text messaging.
G. the number of text messages sent daily allowed her to win a national championship.
H. a teen can accomplish a great deal in just one day.
J. the number of texts in a given day can quickly add up.

19. In line 55, the word *assayed* most nearly means:

A. examined.
B. reasoned.
C. estimated.
D. wrote.

20. The author would most likely agree that:

F. SMS technology is causing more harm for humanity than good.
G. all technology should be limited to those who are responsible.
H. SMS technology is the current pinnacle of telecommunications.
J. as technology develops, the people of the world are being brought closer together.

Movies and music can define a generation and become cultural phenomena, and YouTube has helped do that for this generation. Teens and millennials in the U.S. are the highest users of the web giant with more than 80% and 70% respectively using the site regularly. With these two groups accounting for the majority of users and the U.S. making up approximately 20% of the user base of the site, it is no wonder why certain videos have become YouTube's most viewed of all time.

YouTube often releases information, typically at the end of each year, about its most popular videos, but one only needs to look at a specific video to learn just how many views it has had since it was posted. It is obvious that videos posted earlier have an advantage over newer videos, but that hasn't stopped some recent additions from skyrocketing up the list. One such music video that has reached such fame is Katy Perry and Juicy J's "Dark Horse." In about a year and a half, the video has earned the third spot of all time views with over one billion views since its addition to YouTube on February 20, 2014. Watch out, though, Katy, because Taylor Swift's "Blank Space" resides in the fourth spot approaching one billion views. Though it has an eight month deficit in posting date, this is quickly becoming insignificant.

Love it or hate it, one of the oldest videos to still reside on the top charts is Justin Bieber's "Baby." Around since early 2010, the then teen sensation has garnered 1.2 billion views to make it the second ranking YouTube video of all time. Despite its apparent popularity, "Baby" has nearly five million dislikes, surpassing its three million likes.

Residing at the number one spot of YouTube's all time most viewed videos, one that currently averages just under one million views daily, is Psy's "Gangnam Style." Uploaded in July 2012, it has been viewed 2.35 billion times from users all over the world. That averages to approximately 788 million views a year! That yearly average is better than the all-time totals of these extremely popular videos: Carly Rae Jepsen's "Call Me Maybe," Macklemore & Ryan Lewis's "Thrift Shop," and Miley Cyrus's "Wrecking Ball." To say Psy has done something incredible is an understatement; however, it is just a matter of time before another video overtakes Psy's number one ranking.

Another popular category on YouTube is the video game genre. With over 38 million subscribers, PewDiePie combines video game gameplay with a sense of juvenile, obnoxious humor and unique, high pitched screams that just may be the secret to success on YouTube. VanossGaming features many videos of funny moments while playing various games with friends and comes in with 13 million subscribers. With similar commentary and gameplay as the higher ranking gamers, Sky Does Minecraft is the third most subscribed video game channel featuring the very popular Minecraft (Minecraft is actually the second most searched keyword on YouTube).

It doesn't always take musical fame or video gaming with friends to create a YouTube sensation. One of the top videos of all time is "Charlie Bit My Finger – Again!" and features a family who was quite ordinary until sudden viral fame hit with one memorable chomp. 830 million people have made Charlie and his brother famous! "Evolution of Dance," posted by Judson Laipply, is approaching 300 million views in the near decade it has been available. In the video, Laipply dances in different styles to songs of all generations. "David After Dentist" features a 7 year old boy who is just coming out of anesthesia and can't exactly act normal. Finally, "Talking Twin Babies – Part 2" shows exactly what one would expect—babbling babies in a nonsense conversation with one another. None of these very normal people were looking for fame—it simply found them!

Famed artist Andy Warhol once said, "In the future, everyone will be world famous for 15 minutes." He certainly didn't know it, but YouTube is just the vehicle for this kind of quick fame. Whether by posting the next viral video, striving for millions of subscribers, or giving the people of the world their favorite songs, YouTube has made it possible for people of all walks of life to become famous, if only for a moment.

21. It can be reasonably inferred that the author thinks PewDiePie's commentary is:

A. annoying.
B. innovative.
C. boring.
D. inspirational.

22. Based on information in the passage, which group views YouTube videos most frequently?

F. Gamers.
G. U.S. millennials ages 20-30.
H. Musicians.
J. U.S. teenagers.

23. According to the passage, which of these videos was posted most recently?

A. "Gangnam Style."
B. "Blank Space."
C. "Evolution of Dance."
D. "Dark Horse."

24. What type of writing is demonstrated in the passage?

F. Expository.
G. Persuasive.
H. Narrative.
J. Descriptive.

25. It can reasonably be inferred from the passage that Justin Bieber's song "Baby:"

A. has more haters than fans.
B. is actually supported in rankings by people visiting the song just to click *dislike*.
C. was one of the first music videos uploaded to YouTube.
D. will soon surpass Psy's "Gangnam Style" in the rankings.

26. Which of the following most accurately states the main idea of the sixth paragraph (lines 59-75)?

F. Hidden videos have the best chance of going viral.
G. Babies and kids are the keys to getting a video to go viral.
H. Anyone can become a YouTube sensation.
J. Young children are exploited for the sake of their parents' fame.

27. The word *garnered* as used in like 27 most nearly means:

A. corrupted.
B. loathed.
C. gained.
D. misled.

28. Why would the author most likely include the songs by Jepsen, Macklemore & Ryan Lewis, and Cyrus?

F. Help advertise for some of his favorite artists.
G. Emphasize just how popular Psy's song is by comparing it to other popular songs.
H. Provide details about other songs on YouTube's all-time top ten list.
J. Make a sweeping generalization that these artists are not as talented as Psy.

29. It is reasonable to conclude that the channel Sky Does Minecraft includes all of the following EXCEPT:

A. a humorous style.
B. high pitched screaming.
C. playing games with friends.
D. Minecraft game footage.

30. Based on information in the passage, when was "Blank Space" posted to YouTube?

F. July 2015.
G. February 2014.
H. November 2014.
J. July 2012.

Let's put this into perspective: The Earth has been around for about 4.6 billion years, and if we were to scale this down to an easier-to-comprehend period of 46 years, the human race would have been around for about four hours. The Industrial Revolution that started in the late 18th century would have started about a minute ago, and in that one minute of time, we have done immeasurable and incomprehensible damage to the planet. If we have ransacked, pillaged, and stripped the planet in order to attain fuels, minerals, and room for our exploding human population in such a short period of time, what does the future hold for our home? It is predicted that at this rate of growth, the human race will have three times as many people as today by the year 2100, and for a planet that has already reached its breaking point long ago, we are simply a plague invading and infesting the planet. We produce so much waste that it is not only filling the land, but also floating on the ocean in a garbage patch that could be, by varying estimates, the size of a small island or as big as twice the size of the United States. Our water and air are constantly being tainted, so how long could our infected, decaying earth sustain a human population? It's time to act, not only for the governments and corporations, but to make up for the immensity of harm, each individual should also. "Going green" may seem like a buzz word for "everyone but me," but it simply isn't an option anymore. Our planet, the home we all share, demands it.

Human population growth can be attributed to a few major factors: improved food production, better public health, and medical advances. Improved survival rate means people are living longer and surviving when diseases or malnutrition would have previously killed them. Though seemingly a good thing, this resilience has put an incredible strain on the planet. With a larger population, living accommodations must be met, which means spreading out. This in turn means less natural land (home to vegetation that allows us to breathe!) and land to feed that population. A larger population means, among other concerns, increased waste and use of environmentally harmful products. The earth will not be able to provide for an exponentially growing population with limited resources and limited space. Will mass starvation occur around the world in the near future due to food shortages caused by increased population? The question is not will it happen, but when will it happen?

Though worldwide population growth is a major concern, reducing pollution is not out of our hands. Certainly people of all nations share in the responsibility to cut pollution, but Americans should feel even more responsible. Why? Because if the entire world lived as wastefully and carelessly as Americans do, we would need four planets to hold all our waste, meet our insatiable need for natural resources, and absorb all our pollution. Americans use 2.5 million plastic bottles every hour, and the majority of those bottles are used once and thrown away. Just Americans! Every two weeks, Americans use enough glass bottles and jars to fill a skyscraper, and in a year, we waste so much paper that a twelve foot wall could be constructed from New York to Seattle! We consume 50 million tons of paper annually, which is the equivalent of 850 million trees. Our own wasteful habits are destroying the Earth.

By recycling these products, we can reduce the raw materials needed to produce these goods. Every ton of recycled paper not only reduces the strain on landfills, but saves 380 gallons of oil. Glass produced from recycled glass instead of raw materials decreases air pollution by 20% and water pollution by 50%. For every ton of plastic recycled (approximately 38,000 20-ounce bottles), we save 2000 pounds of oil, enough energy for two people's consumption for a year, and one person's water use for two months. These everyday objects account for only a fraction of things that can be recycled; it is estimated that 60% of consumer waste can be recycled. Saving resources while reducing the pollution of our air, water, and land must become a priority in all our lives, because, after all, we don't have four Earths to play scapegoat for our careless living behaviors.

Though the situation is dire, changes to our everyday habits can have an immediate and immense impact on our world. We must start looking at our actions as a chain of events that have far-reaching effects. For example, think about your daily use of water. Using excess water when showering, washing dishes, doing laundry, or even brushing teeth extends to the amount of water going through water processing plants and the energy used to treat it, not to mention the raw and refined chemicals used to clean it. The waste water must then be treated and go through sewage plants. Your own gas or electric water heater uses more natural gas or electricity (produced by various means, but most likely by the natural resources coal or natural gas), which uses unnecessary resources. Yes, simply running the hot water in the shower for a few extra minutes a day will create a large ripple. We can do some simple things to decrease our impact on the environment, but we must start immediately. Think about your choices every day, for it is imperative to start taking better care of our earth now or one day soon it will not be able to take the fall for our careless living.

31. The author's tone throughout the passage can best be described as:

A. apathetic.
B. idealistic.
C. forthright.
D. hesitant.

32. The intended purpose of the passage is most likely to:

F. inform.
G. persuade.
H. entertain.
J. sadden.

33. The author states in paragraph two (lines 29-46) that when population increases, all of the following occur EXCEPT:

A. a strain on natural resources.
B. mass extinction from a lack of food.
C. a greater amount of waste is produced.
D. a greater demand for land for housing.

34. Which of the following is NOT likely a possible purpose of including the example of excess water usage in the last paragraph (lines 80-100)?

F. Bring to light individual wasteful habits and how they can have wide effects.
G. Encourage readers to take cold showers in order to save energy.
H. Suggest an example with which readers can relate.
J. Convince readers to think about everyday living habits and alter them.

35. As it is used in line 48, the phrase "out of our hands" most nearly means:

A. an area an individual cannot control.
B. the act of releasing litter.
C. a subject that is not the concern of an individual.
D. a recyclable alternative.

36. The intended audience of the passage is most likely:

F. an individual seeking specific ways to change industries' destructive methods.
G. a high school student seeking knowledge for a "go green" research report.
H. an American citizen in search of practical alternatives to common pollutants.
J. an individual interested in the environmental concerns plaguing the earth and possible solutions.

37. The passage indicates in paragraph three (lines 47-63) that 850 million trees are enough to:

A. save 380 gallons of oil if the paper made from them is properly recycled.
B. create a wall of paper that stretches across the nation.
C. build a skyscraper in New York.
D. satisfy the world's needs for magazines, newspapers, and office paper for a year.

38. It can reasonably be inferred from the first paragraph (lines 1-28) that the author feels human beings:

F. should have never allowed the Industrial Revolution to begin.
G. will be at war for land and food by 2100.
H. are parasites that will kill their host.
J. do not deserve to live on this Earth.

39. Which of the following did the author clearly intend to show in the passage through the logical progression from all mankind, to Americans, to the individual?

A. Though environmental problems are caused globally, there are things a mere individual can do to reduce the plundering and destruction of the planet.
B. The general-to-specific construction resembles a film in which the camera displays the global destruction and quickly zooms in to the continent, city, and then street of the individual causing the problem.
C. All play a role in destroying the earth, but the American people care least about solving the issues.
D. A general-to-specific structural approach strengthens the idea that every single individual on the planet must be identified as a cause to and solution for environmental woes.

40. It can be reasonably inferred from the statement "home to vegetation that allows us to breathe!" (lines 37-38) that natural land:

F. is an area in which humans can retreat in order to breathe fresh air.
G. is an escape from the ever-increasing cramped living quarters.
H. houses natural vegetation that we can eat without farming, thus, keeping us alive.
J. houses the plants that convert carbon dioxide to oxygen.

Test 3

ENGLISH

75 questions

45 minutes

ANSWER SHEET-ENGLISH TEST 3

1.____   16.____   31.____   46.____   61.____

2.____   17.____   32.____   47.____   62.____

3.____   18.____   33.____   48.____   63.____

4.____   19.____   34.____   49.____   64.____

5.____   20.____   35.____   50.____   65.____

6.____   21.____   36.____   51.____   66.____

7.____   22.____   37.____   52.____   67.____

8.____   23.____   38.____   53.____   68.____

9.____   24.____   39.____   54.____   69.____

10.____   25.____   40.____   55.____   70.____

11.____   26.____   41.____   56.____   71.____

12.____   27.____   42.____   57.____   72.____

13.____   28.____   43.____   58.____   73.____

14.____   29.____   44.____   59.____   74.____

15.____   30.____   45.____   60.____   75.____

College Athletes

Fans decked out in jerseys with their favorite

(1)player's number's file into the massive stadium,

eager to cheer on **(2)its** team. The head coach **(3)and a**

multi-millionaire paces the sidelines, flanked by

television cameras and sportscasters, who have paid

handsomely **(4)for the rights to** broadcast the game.

The crowd cheers as the players run onto the field.

(5)Yet these players, the center of all this attention and

admiration, are likely eating ramen noodles for dinner.

This is a scene from a typical college football

game. **(6)In accordance with** National Collegiate

Athletic Association (NCAA) regulations, student

athletes are not allowed to receive compensation for

their athletic abilities.

1. A. NO CHANGE
    B. players' numbers
    C. player's numbers'
    D. players number's

2. F. NO CHANGE
    G. his or her
    H. their
    J. that

3. A. NO CHANGE
    B. who happens to be extremely rich
    C. is overpaid and
    D. , a multi-millionaire,

4. The underlined portion can be replaced with all of the following EXCEPT:
    F. in order to
    G. to
    H. for the ability to
    J. for the privilege of

5. Which option would NOT be an appropriate replacement for the underlined portion?
    A. However,
    B. Conversely,
    C. Ultimately,
    D. On the other hand,

6. Which of the following options is LEAST acceptable?
    F. Because of
    G. Due to
    H. As a result of
    J. As there are

Some college athletes believe this rule is **(7)dumb** and should be changed, pointing out the large amounts of revenue that **(8)everyone generates** for the university.

Broadcasting contracts alone for the NCAA can run over six billion dollars, not to mention the additional revenue brought in through merchandising. In many respects, the life of a college athlete is very similar **(9)to those of** a professional athlete: **(10)intense workouts, morning-to-night practices, and then having to study playbooks.** On top of the pressure to perform on the field, college athletes have one additional responsibility that the pros do not face: having to fit in class and studying. **(11)On the flip side**, many top college coaches receive salaries that rival the pros, often topping a million dollars a year.

However, some people argue that college athletes should continue to be treated as amateurs. Only about 1% of college athletes end up going **(12)pro and for that reason,** some say, their top focus should be on

7. Which of the following word choices would be most acceptable, considering the style and tone of the passage?
    A. NO CHANGE
    B. unfair
    C. disrespectful
    D. tolerable

8.
    F. NO CHANGE
    G. college athletes make
    H. the NCAA generate
    J. it makes

9.
    A. NO CHANGE
    B. to that of
    C. to
    D. OMIT the underlined portion

10.
    F. NO CHANGE
    G. intense workouts, morning-to-night practices, and playbooks to study.
    H. intensely working out, practicing nightly, and studying playbooks.
    J. intense morning-to-night practices and playbooks.

11.
    A. NO CHANGE
    B. In contrast,
    C. What is not fair is that
    D. OMIT the underlined portion (capitalizing *many*).

12.
    F. NO CHANGE
    G. pro: for that reason,
    H. pro, therefore,
    J. pro. That is why,

earning a degree, **(13)not to make money.** Also, not

every college sport is profitable, and the funds from

larger sports programs, like football and basketball,

(14)is used to underwrite smaller programs, including

track and gymnastics. **[15]**

13. A. NO CHANGE
     B. instead of looking to get rich quick.
     C. rather than to go pro.
     D. not a paycheck.

14. F. NO CHANGE
     G. should be used to
     H. could be used to
     J. are used to

15. Which of the following would be the most appropriate
     closing for this passage?

     A. People care more about football and basketball,
     though.
     B. Overall, it is unfair and unacceptable for the
     talents of student athletes to continue to be exploited
     in this way.
     C. Whatever the case may be, for the time being, it
     appears that the emphasis will continue to be on the
     student aspect of the term student-athlete.
     D. Track and gymnastics programs deserve
     adequate funding.

Pranked

Prom. Graduation. The epidemic known as

"senioritis." These are all **(16)common, ordinary**

features of the senior year of high school. Another

(17)increasingly popular part of senior year is the senior

class prank. **(18)Although** school officials are quick to

discourage these pranks, often times seniors aim to

create funny and memorable moments that will live on

in school history.

The ideas are **(19)boundless. Especially** thanks

to an MTV program chronicling some of the most

creative pranks. The show, **(20)appropriately** titled

Pranked, received a great deal of criticism when it aired.

Some argued that the show promoted vandalism and

(21)it disrupted the learning environment, while others

thought the clip-show format was trite and overdone.

The show, however, did help bring attention to pranking.

16.　F. NO CHANGE
　　　G. typical
　　　H. to be expected
　　　J. run of the mill

17.　A. NO CHANGE
　　　B. important and
　　　C. monumentally
　　　D. definitively

18. Which of the following is NOT an appropriate replacement for the underlined portion?
　　　F. While
　　　G. Though
　　　H. But
　　　J. Even if

19.　A. NO CHANGE
　　　B. boundless; especially
　　　C. boundless, especially
　　　D. boundless especially,

20.　F. NO CHANGE
　　　G. strangely
　　　H. obviously
　　　J. which of course is

21.　A. NO CHANGE
　　　B. the disruption of
　　　C. can be disrupting to
　　　D. disrupted

Some of the best pranks, though, do not need promotion via TV shows or **(22)the internet; Often** times, **(23)it spreads** simply through word of mouth.

One classic prank involves animals, but the joke is less **(24)on** the animals than on the people who spend the day tracking them down.   Students unleash three **(25)** **animals (such as pigs or goats),** each one wearing a numbered tag. When the creatures, labeled #1, #2, and #4 are caught, officials **(26)spend** the rest of the day in search of #3, which does not exist.

Of course, what sounds funny in theory can turn out to be quite **(27) intense.**   For instance, a school in Pennsylvania suffered a security scare when two students posed as custodians. The school received reports of intruders, causing a lockdown and a police search of the building.   The pranksters were subsequently arrested.

(28)Additionally, an Indiana high school student faced up to eight years in prison after a prank turned into a bomb scare. He put a blow-up doll in the girls' bathroom, but when security cameras caught

22. F. NO CHANGE
G. the internet, often
H. the internet; often,
J. the internet; often

23. A. NO CHANGE
B. they spread
C. they'll spread
D. it's spread

24. F. NO CHANGE
G. for
H. about
J. concerning

25. Which of the substitutions for the underlined portion is LEAST acceptable?
A. animals, such as pigs or goats,
B. animals like pigs or goats
C. animals—usually pigs or goats—
D. animals (pigs, goats, etc.),

26. Suppose the writer intends to convey the gullibility of the people involved in the joke. The best way to phrase the underlined portion would be:
F. stupidly spend
G. unconsciously spend
H. reluctantly spend
J. unwittingly spend

27. A. NO CHANGE
B. serious.
C. dull.
D. dangerous.

28. Which of the following options could NOT replace the underlined portion?
F. Similarly,
G. Conversely,
H. Also,
J. Likewise,

footage of a masked man sneaking into the school and hiding a package, school officials became nervous and called the bomb squad to investigate. **[29]**

While some students may feel that administrators overreact to harmless jokes, it is important to remember the safety and well-being of an entire school when planning a senior prank. Are a few laughs and a chance to leave a legacy worth the embarrassment, risk, or possible punishment? That's up for debate, but one thing is for sure—senior year is a chance to make fun, long-lasting memories. **[30]**

29. Suppose the author was considering adding in the following statement:

Even when they realized it was not a bomb, the school still decided to press charges anyway; some people just can't take a joke.

Should the author make this addition?

- A. YES, because it explains the outcome of the story.
- B. YES, because it emphasizes that these pranks are jokes and they are not intended to cause harm.
- C. NO, because it does not consider the school's side of the story.
- D. NO, because it strays from the unbiased, factual tone of the passage.

30. Suppose the author was assigned to write an article about the best senior pranks of the year. Does this passage fulfill that purpose?

F. YES, because it gives examples of two specific pranks.

G. YES, because it discusses a commonly copied prank, as well as a prank that made headlines.

H. NO, because it is more of a general overview of the pros and cons of attempting a senior prank.

J. NO, because the pranks listed here are not clever.

Reality Horror

[1]

A horror movie is made by a young and unknown creator. It is shot on digital video **(31)in a style intentionally giving the impression** that the **(32)movie's principal character's** are the ones filming **(33), not a director**. The characters are played by **(34)relatively, but soon-to-be-famous, unknown actors.** The film plays before small audiences on the festival circuit, gaining praise and infamy with each screening.

[2]

(35)If you stop right there, you could be describing either the *Paranormal Activity* franchise or **(36)the film** *The Blair Witch Project. Paranormal Activity* became the runaway multi-million dollar success that *The Blair Witch Project* was ten years previously. It also became a revitalizing force for **(37) it's** genre in the same way.

31. A. NO CHANGE
     B. in a style intentional giving the impression
     C. in an intentional style to giving the impression
     D. with style intentions of giving the impression

32. F. NO CHANGE
     G. movies principal characters
     H. movie's principal characters
     J. movies' principal characters'

33. The best placement for the underlined portion is:
     A. where it is now.
     B. after the word *character's* (replacing the period with a comma).
     C. after the word *that* (replacing the period with a comma).
     D. OMIT the underlined portion

34. F. NO CHANGE
     G. famous but unknown actors.
     H. relatively unknown actors.
     J. unknown actors.

35. A. NO CHANGE
     B. If you stop right there. You
     C. If you stop, there you
     D. If you stop right there you

36. Suppose the writer wanted to convey the idea that *The Blair Witch Project* paved the way for films like *Paranormal Activity.* Which word choice would best accomplish this?

     F. NO CHANGE
     G. its companion,
     H. its predecessor,
     J. its inspiration,

37. A. NO CHANGE
     B. their
     C. its
     D. its'

[3]

When it was released in the summer of 1999, Daniel Myrick and Eduardo Sanchez's *The Blair Witch Project* was a revelation for horror cinema. The 1990s, a bad decade for **(38)scary movies, were worth forgetting**. The vast majority of those that saw a wide release were echoes of '80s slasher classics or high-numbered sequels to old franchises **(39)like** *Friday the 13th* and *Halloween*. **[40]**

[4]

It's telling that the most successful horror film of the decade was one that satirized the genre. *Scream* (1996) was fundamentally about how stale horror cinema had become. A combination of factors made *Blair Witch* effective three years later: its then-revolutionary multimedia viral marketing, its intentional amateur presentation, and the resulting perceived authenticity. **[41]**

[5]

Blair Witch didn't birth **(42)many imitators but** it did stir up enough public interest for studios to at least try to find more original horror films for release. *The Ring* (2002) spurred a number of hugely successful new horror movies, leading to a flood of American

38.   F. NO CHANGE
      G. scary movies, was worth forgetting.
      H. scary movies—were worth forgetting.
      J. scary movies was worth forgetting.

39.   A. NO CHANGE
      B. like,
      C. like—
      D. like;

40. For the sake of unity and coherence, Paragraph 3 should be placed:
      F. where it is now.
      G. after paragraph 1
      H. after paragraph 4
      J. after paragraph 5

41. Which of the following sentences, if added at the end of Paragraph 4, would most effectively conclude the subject of the paragraph?

      A. *Blair Witch* had little known actors (at the time) playing their roles fantastically.
      B. More than that, though, the movie was legitimately scary in the way it built suspense.
      C. There was nothing like seeing *Blair Witch* for the first time in a crowded, dark theater.
      D. Viewers of *Paranormal Activity* say that it is unique in its presentation, which is not true.

42.   F. NO CHANGE
      G. many imitators; but
      H. many imitators and
      J. many imitators, but

(43)remaking of Japanese horror films, while *Saw*

(2003) popularized the "torture" subgenre of horror.

43. A. NO CHANGE
     B. remakes
     C. additions
     D. sequels

[6]

Unfortunately, studios seem to operate under the assumption that audiences are hungry for more of the same. As a result, we're mired in a **(44)deep** pool of old ideas that, while still having an audience, are failing to excite and spook in the way **(45)it** once did. It will be interesting to see if the old formula of "reality horror" will manage to engage audiences and excite the industry the way it did more than a decade ago.

44. Suppose the author wished to convey the idea that the new crop of horror movies is tired and boring. The best word choice to complete the analogy would be:

     F. NO CHANGE
     G. restless
     H. stagnant
     J. repugnant

45. A. NO CHANGE
     B. we
     C. they
     D. these

PASSAGE IV

Flash Mobs

[1]

This is just one example of the modern phenomenon known as a flash mob.   The term **(46) that was coined in 2003,** is used to describe a large gathering of people in a public space **(47)for no clear purpose.** Mobbers are often decked out in costume and spontaneously dance to a **(48)surprisingly** well-choreographed routine. **(49)We** enjoy being part of the group and getting attention from onlookers.

46.   F. NO CHANGE
      G. , having been coined in 2003,
      H. which was coined in 2003,
      J. OMIT the underlined portion

47. The best placement for the underlined portion is:
      A. where it is now.
      B. after the word *gathering*
      C. after the word *describe*
      D. OMIT the underlined portion

48. Should the author delete the underlined portion?
      F. YES, because it makes the sentence too wordy.
      G. YES, because that fact is not surprising.
      H. NO, because it serves as a contrast to the seemingly spontaneous nature of flash mobs.
      J. NO, because it explains flash mobs' popularity.

49.   A. NO CHANGE
      B. They
      C. Participants
      D. The audience

[2]

Pillow fights are a common occurrence at slumber parties **(50)and** recently more and more adults (hundreds, in fact) **(51)were joining** in on the fun. In

50.   F. NO CHANGE
      G. , but
      H. , however,
      J. while

51.   A. NO CHANGE
      B. are joining
      C. will have joined
      D. will join

Shanghai, **(52)designed to allow participants to blow off some steam and relieve some stress**, college students and office workers gather for a massive pillow fight.

52. The best placement for the underlined portion is:
    F. where it is now
    G. after the word *students* (replacing the comma with a period)
    H. after the word *gather* (replacing the comma with a period)
    J. after the word *fight* (replacing the comma with a period)

[3]

The technique of flash mobbing has taken on a more significant meaning at times **(53)as** Occupy Wall Street protestors have used the approach to garner attention for their cause. In 2011, protestors in Chicago made headlines when they stormed the city wearing Robin Hood costumes **(54)and they kayaked across the Chicago River.** What was once an unusual occurrence is, ironically, becoming **(55)somewhat of the norm**. Don't be surprised to see a flash mob at a local mall near you.

53.   A. NO CHANGE
    B. with
    C. though
    D. OMIT the underlined portion

54.   F. NO CHANGE
    G. as they kayaked across the Chicago River.
    H. but kayaking across the Chicago River.
    J. in the Chicago River, where they rowed kayaks.

55. Which replacement for the underlined portion is LEAST acceptable?
    A. normal.
    B. expected.
    C. rather ordinary.
    D. boring.

The mobs were originally intended to poke fun

at **(56)and mock** organized protests and people's need to

conform. **(57)In fact,** the popularity of this fad had

the opposite effect. Advertisers **(58)are using** the

approach to garner free publicity. For instance, cell

phone provider T- Mobile organized flash mobs that

were later incorporated into the **(59)companies**

television commercials. The trend was even the subject

of a storyline on the popular ABC comedy *Modern

Family.* **[60]**

56.   F. NO CHANGE
      G. or mock
      H. or make a commentary about
      J. OMIT the underlined portion

57.   A. NO CHANGE
      B. However,
      C. Regardless,
      D. Meanwhile,

58.   F. NO CHANGE
      G. may soon be using
      H. using
      J. used

59.   A. NO CHANGE
      B. companies'
      C. company's
      D. companys'

60. The most logical order for the paragraphs is this passage
     is:
      F. 1, 2, 3, 4
      G. 2, 1, 4, 3
      H. 2, 4, 3, 1
      J. 3, 2, 4, 1

Young Money

Lil Wayne is one of the most popular entertainers today. When Dwayne Michael Carter, Jr. was **(61)growing up, he was a straight-A, intelligent, student,** who loved to express himself through music. At the age of 11, he got his foot in the door at the Cash Money record label. The **(62)experience needless to say** opened up many doors. In 1997 he dropped the "D" from his first name, going by Lil Wayne. **(63)Double platinum, Lil Wayne released his first solo album** two years later **(64)in 1999** and **(65)would release** a second album in 2000. Titled *Lights Out*, the sophomore effort failed to match the success **(66)of the freshmen effort.**

Lil Wayne achieved a wider audience after the release of his underground mix tape. This led to the follow-up album *Tha Carter*. The rhymes he laid on the tracks showed significant growth, and **(67)when** he was featured on the Destiny's Child track "Soldier," he

61.   A. NO CHANGE
B. growing up, he was a straight-A, intelligent student
C. growing up, he was a straight-A intelligent, student
D. growing up he was a straight-A intelligent student,

62.   F. NO CHANGE
G. experience
H. experience, needless to say,
J. experience can be said to have

63.   A. NO CHANGE
B. Lil Wayne released double platinum his first solo album
C. Lil Wayne double platinum released his first solo album
D. Lil Wayne released his first double platinum solo album

64.   F. NO CHANGE
G. after 1997
H. before 2000
J. OMIT the underlined portion

65.   A. NO CHANGE
B. released
C. had released
D. was releasing

66.   F. NO CHANGE
G. then the original album.
H. of its predecessor.
J. OMIT the underlined portion.

67.   A. NO CHANGE
B. while,
C. even though,
D. ,thus, when

almost **(68) instant** earned the status of a mainstream

artist. His talent, **(69)in which it** was often overlooked

by middle America, was finally being recognized. **[70]**

Soon, Wayne's popularity grew in mainstream

music, on DJ mix tapes, and on the internet. *Tha Carter*

II became a major music industry event, selling over a

quarter-million copies the first week of its release and

later going platinum. Two tracks featured Robin Thicke,

and the album also introduced audiences to

(71)Wayne's, Young Money, crew. With no release

date for the **(72)albums follow-up** in sight, fans could

only settle for Lil Wayne's guest appearances on other

artists' tracks.

Finally, *Tha Carter III* arrived in May of 2008,

selling more than a million copies in its first week of

(73)release. Spawning a slew of number one singles.

The album earned Wayne four Grammy Awards and led

to appearances on *Saturday Night Live* and the Country

68. F. NO CHANGE
G. more instantly
H. nearly instantly
J. instantly

69. A. NO CHANGE
B. that
C. which
D. OMIT the underlined portion

70. Which of the following sentences, if added here, would best reflect the point made in this paragraph?

F. Lil Wayne is the best rapper ever!
G. Lil Wayne continued to evolve as an artist, allowing him to reach new audiences.
H. Destiny's Child front woman Beyonce' is married to Jay-Z.
J. Many Chicagoans like Lil Wayne.

71. A. NO CHANGE
B . Wayne's Young Money, crew.
C. Wayne's, Young Money crew.
D. Wayne's Young Money crew.

72. F. NO CHANGE
G. album's follow-up
H. albums's follow-up
J. albums' follow-up

73. A. NO CHANGE
B. release! Spawning
C. release; spawning
D. release, spawning

Music Awards. **[74]**

74. Suppose the writer wanted to conclude this paragraph by emphasizing Lil Wayne's cross-genre appeal. Which sentence would best accomplish this purpose?

F. Lil Wayne decided to release a country album to garner more fans.
G. These appearances cemented Lil Wayne's appeal amongst a wide range of audiences.
H. Lil Wayne decided to try his hand at comedy by appearing in several *SNL* sketches.
J. Pretty much everyone likes Lil Wayne's music.

In 2010, Wayne released a rock-oriented album, *Rebirth*, but the music was overshadowed by Wayne's prison sentence for weapons charges. Fans stuck by him, though, and when *Tha Carter IV* was released **(75)** **in 2011. Lil Wayne soon** found his way back on the airwaves. There seems to be nothing stopping Dwayne Michael Carter, Jr.

75. A. NO CHANGE
B. in 2011; Lil Wayne soon
C. in 2011, and Lil Wayne soon
D. in 2011, Lil Wayne soon

END OF ENGLISH TEST 3

Test 3

READING

40 questions

35 minutes

ANSWER SHEET- READING TEST 3

1.____   11.____   21.____   31.____

2.____   12.____   22.____   32.____

3.____   13.____   23.____   33.____

4.____   14.____   24.____   34.____

5.____   15.____   25.____   35.____

6.____   16.____   26.____   36.____

7.____   17.____   27.____   37.____

8.____   18.____   28.____   38.____

9.____   19.____   29.____   39.____

10.____   20.____   30.____   40.____

"That night I felt like I had to tell everyone. If Stacy was going to say things like that, I had to tell all of our friends so they know what kind of a person she really is. I Tweeted that Stacy can't be trusted with secrets; she'll tell. I put my phone down, went to sleep, and came to school this morning. In math she didn't talk to me, and in English she gave me hard looks. Then at lunch, she sat somewhere else instead of with all of us. Everyone was talking about us, but I wasn't really listening. Then Beth Driscoll ran up to me when I was finishing my fries and said that Stacy wanted to fight after school. This was a real surprise to me; I had no intention of actually fighting, but when all of my friends were looking at me waiting for a response, I couldn't back down. I told Beth to tell her that I would meet her a block away from school on Moody Street and we'd solve our issue. We walked down that block to get home anyway.

"The rest of the day, I didn't see Stacy, but I grew increasingly nervous. I didn't want to fight her—I only wanted people to know that Stacy is a blabbermouth and can't be trusted. We've been friends for like ten years, ever since Kindergarten. I trusted her with secrets all the time, but she's changed. If she told everyone my secret, it's obvious she doesn't respect our friendship anymore.

"After school, a whole group of people followed me down to Moody. I heard everyone talking about how I was going to kick her butt and I better not back down. I was really nervous—she's my best friend and I didn't want to fight her—but everyone had their phones out ready to take videos. I know what happens to those videos; they show up on YouTube for like the whole world to see. I thought about how to get out of it, but with a crowd of people around, I doubted that I could. My own reputation was on the line. I was going to have to fight Stacy, but I don't know why she felt she had to fight me. All I did was tell everyone the truth about her and how she can't keep a secret. I never saw this side of her—she's a bully who wanted to punch my face in.

"I walked down the next block and see a huge crowd with her, too. I heard people yelling in anticipation. I saw Stacy at the same time she saw me. I looked down to the ground right as soon as our eyes met.

"Stacy started mumbling something right away, but her words were drowned out by the mob. They were all shouting, their phones and cameras were out, and they made a circle around us. My pounding heart told me I didn't want to do it, but I really didn't have a choice. I thought to myself, 'I wish someone would stop us. I even hope someone would call our parents or the cops or someone.' Just then, someone pulled off my backpack and pushed me into Stacy. She pushed me back, hard! The crowd erupted with *oooh*s. Now I was angry, so I pushed her back just as hard. Everyone around us shouted again. The push sent Stacy back into the circle, and I saw people shoving her at me. It wasn't right. This fight was being run by this group of kids. Most of them I don't even talk to. Why did they want to see us fight so badly? So they can pretend to be cool when people comment on their YouTube video? This whole thing had gotten way out of hand. I saw her head kind of jerk back from someone's shove and she flew into me and fell at my feet. I didn't push her down—it was the force with which some kid pushed her that made her lose her balance. She turned her head and looked up at me and I saw a tear fall from her sad eyes. The crowd shouted 'Come on, hit her!' and 'Kick her butt,' but just as I reached down to help her up, I heard a man shouting and saw from the corner of my eye the dean pushing through the crowd.

"You grabbed both of us by our coats, sir, and you brought us here. That's the story. Stacy just wanted to bully me because I told the truth."

The dean sighed. I had never been in the dean's office before—I always thought it would look more like a jail than a warm and cozy little room with pictures of his family next to his computer. Stacy was staring down at the table at which we were both sitting. I knew she felt bad for bullying me—she's just changed, that's all. I hoped right then that the dean would give her the punishment she deserved, and then we could be friends again after that, if she tried to make it all up to me, that is.

The dean asked, "Stacy, you want to tell your side of the story?" Stacy meekly nodded her head and got up and went to the dean's computer. She pulled up her Twitter account and started pointing to some comments. The dean put on his glasses, inched closer to the screen, and squinted.

Stacy said, "See, look at all the mean comments people wrote about me since last night. 'I hate you,' 'Stacy, you're such a'…uh, bad word there," she hesitated. "It fills up the whole page." Stacy started crying. The

95 dean took the mouse and skimmed through the comments, then turned his head and looked over at me and shook his head disappointingly. "Everyone hates me now! I had to eat lunch alone, and then some people even started rumors that I wanted to fight. I didn't want
100 to fight, and I never said I would. Other kids just said whatever they wanted about me. A whole crowd of people followed me down the block and called me chicken and bad names. I had to make them stop, so I waited for Lauren, hoping that she wouldn't want to fight, either."
105 Stacy then turned toward me but didn't look up. "I'm sorry! I didn't mean to tell anyone that you liked Dan, but when I saw him really staring at you yesterday, I thought he should know you liked him, too. I was trying to help!" Stacy broke down into heartfelt sobs.

110 The dean stared into my soul and said, "I never took you for a bully, Lauren. This is just awful."

I realized what I had done. I could do nothing but stare at my shaking fingers and nervously pick at my nail polish while wanting so badly to get up and hug
115 Stacy and tell her with all my heart I was so sorry, but even if I did, things would never be the same again.

1. It can be reasonably inferred that Stacy pushes the narrator with great force (line 53) for all of the following reasons EXCEPT:

A. Stacy reacts to the crowd's urging.
B. Stacy takes her chance to start the fight.
C. Stacy feels she must defend herself.
D. Stacy feels the narrator shouldn't have pushed her.

2. It can be reasonably inferred that author includes information about the dean's office (lines 76-78) in order to:

F. suggest the dean wants visitors to feel uncomfortable when entering.
G. identify that this dean is unimportant due to having a small office.
H. provide some imagery to the plain passage.
J. suggest the dean has feelings and human emotions.

3. Which of the following is a reasonable conclusion the reader can draw about the events that likely occur after the passage ends?

A. Stacy is ostracized by others at her school.
B. Stacy works to fix their friendship.
C. The narrator is expelled from school.
D. The narrator and Stacy finish their fight.

4. Stacy can most accurately be characterized as:

F. stalwart and unwavering.
G. depressed and dejected.
H. egotistical and self-centered.
J. perplexed and baffled.

5. The author clearly intends to show all of the following through the writing of this passage EXCEPT:

A. that people should keep secrets to themselves.
B. the growing concerns of cyberbullying.
C. how a group can influence an individual.
D. the unintended consequences of posting information online.

6. The narrator's point of view is that of:

F. an omniscient protagonist.
G. a biased character.
H. an objective observer.
J. a concealing individual.

7. As used in the passage, the line "stared into my soul" (line 110) can be understood to mean:

A. the dean knows that she is not a bully deep down.
B. the dean wishes to see the narrator's reaction to Stacy's tears.
C. the dean studies the narrator for her true character.
D. the dean employs a technique used by authority figures to make their suspect speak the truth.

8. The author suggests that the two friends actually confront each other due to:

F. friendly encouragement by the group.
G. psychological and physical pressure from the mob.
H. Stacy's need to take the issue to the physical level.
J. the narrator's desire to settle a disagreement.

9. One can reasonably infer from the passage that the narrator's goal in posting details on Twitter is to:

A. give a status update.
B. end a friendship.
C. torment a friend.
D. avenge slighted feelings.

10. It can be reasonably inferred that the line "I realized what I had done" (line 112) suggests the narrator knows she is responsible for all of the following EXCEPT:

F. ruining their friendship.
G. being a bully.
H. causing Stacy to feel so upset.
J. creating the mob that urges on the fight.

PASSAGE II—SOCIAL SCIENCE   "Insects in WHAT?"

There is no denying that Americans have a love-hate relationship with food. We love to eat many things that are considered bad for our bodies, sometimes in great quantities. Likewise, many people spend time and money
5 on diets to compensate, while others eat healthy foods daily. Americans may spend time counting calories, but many would be surprised at what the Food and Drug Administration (FDA) is counting. This government agency sets the standards for food handlers and processors, and
10 with it, sets the allowable level of things in food that might surprise and disgust even the savviest consumer. Yes, the FDA sets acceptable levels of things like insect parts, larvae, and rodent filth in the foods we eat every day. How about that for watching what you eat?

15 The FDA publishes and regularly updates the "Defects Levels Handbook," which establishes the allowable levels of "natural or unavoidable defects that present no health hazards for humans." Many sections of the handbook deal with handling specifications, amounts of
20 decomposition allowed, or what percentage of mold or mildew is tolerable. The average consumer has to expect that not everything on the shelves or in the produce department can be absolutely perfect; however, one may not expect contaminants like fly parts and rodent hair. Rest
25 assured, though, that these impurities are harmless, at least in the amounts specified by the FDA, and are considered a matter of aesthetics.

So what are the allowable levels of food contaminants for some of our favorite foods? Let's start with one
30 of our favorite snacks, chocolate. Based on 100 gram samples (about 3.5 ounces), there is an acceptable average of less than sixty insect fragments when six 100-gram samples are examined or any one sample from this group with less than ninety insect parts. Oh wait, there's more!
35 When it comes to rodent contamination, over six 100-gram samples, the average number of rodent hairs must be less than one or any one sample from the group must have less than three rodent hairs. Since the average chocolate bar is about 1.5 ounces, that means that for every two to
40 three bars, one could feasibly be eating up to sixty to ninety insect parts and one or two rodent hairs. Maybe one should think twice the next time a chocolate craving strikes.

Another common food we all snack on from time
45 to time is the movie theater staple, popcorn. In a pound of popcorn, the FDA considers less than two rodent hairs acceptable or less than twenty gnawed grains per pound. Thankfully, if any rodent droppings are found in any sample, the FDA will take action. Thank you, FDA!

50 Peanut butter—the lunchtime favorite. Per 100 grams, an average of thirty or more insect fragments is deemed excessive. But twenty-nine insect bits? Sure, that's fine!

Who doesn't like a good pizza? (Perhaps fewer
55 after reading this.) The pizza sauce contamination limit is twenty-nine fly eggs or one maggot per 100 grams. So, pick your poison—fly eggs or a maggot in your next pizza? I prefer my pizza with cheese only!

According to the FDA, typical foods contain
60 about 10 percent of the levels indicated before action is taken. Others claim the real percentage is closer to 40 percent. Can we ever know how many insect parts are ground up in processing or how many rodent hairs make it through to the things we eat every day? Probably not. An
65 Ohio University study estimates that we eat anywhere from one to two pounds of insects a year without knowing it. Perhaps being unaware of what we're eating may be the best thing for us. Like the maxim says, "Ignorance is bliss."

70 If you are extremely concerned about these facts, you may be wondering, is there anything I can do to avoid eating these contaminants? Becoming more self-sufficient may be part of the solution, but nearly all Americans rely upon processed goods or factory-handled foods for the
75 majority of their food supply. Besides, how many insects land on your home-grown tomatoes and leave behind waste? How many animals would snack on your apples? Adding pesticides to prevent this from happening is likely worse than the insect remnants themselves. Dr. Philip
80 Nixon, an entomologist at the University of Illinois, says that insects are "actually pretty healthy. If we were more willing to accept certain defect levels such as insects and insect parts, growers could reduce pesticide usage." The FDA agrees and states that pesticide exposure to humans
85 is potentially hazardous while the aesthetically unpleasing yet natural and unavoidable defects are harmless. Reducing defect levels to satisfy consumer distaste of insect parts would mean an increase in chemical substances in the food. Consumer preference for fewer pesticides or
90 insect parts may one day influence our entire food supply.

So, the next time you find a fly in your soup, don't be so quick to blame the chef!

11. According to the third paragraph, which of the following would be an acceptable level of food contamination in chocolate samples?

   A. An average of 90 insect parts per six 100-gram sample
   B. A total of 6 rodent hairs per six 100-gram sample
   C. 3 rodent hairs in one 100-gram sample
   D. A total of 300 insect parts per six 100-gram sample

12. According to the passage, who or what approximates that Americans unwittingly eat up to two pounds of insects a year?

   F. Ohio University
   G. Dr. Philip Nixon
   H. The Food and Drug Administration
   J. Entomologists

13. As it is used in line 11, the word *savviest* means:

   A. sarcastic.
   B. perceptive.
   C. crafty.
   D. visionary.

14. It can be reasonably inferred that the FDA would claim that the following number of insect parts in a 100-gram sample of peanut butter could be considered typical:

   F. 2-3
   G. 29
   H. 30
   J. 100

15. It can be reasonably inferred from information in the passage that one way to significantly reduce insect contaminants in an individual's food supply is to:

   A. increase pesticide use on farms.
   B. purchase only locally grown foods.
   C. accept a greater defect level.
   D. grow tomatoes in one's own backyard.

16. The words *aesthetics* (line 27) and *aesthetically* (line 85) mean:

   F. naturally occurring.
   G. unavoidable circumstances.
   H. pleasing to the senses.
   J. harmless material.

17. It can be reasonably inferred that Dr. Philip Nixon (lines 79-80) would likely accept all of the following EXCEPT:

   A. an increase in home-grown foods.
   B. an increase in pesticide use on the food supply.
   C. an increase in insect parts in the food supply.
   D. a decrease in pesticide use on the food supply.

18. The main function of paragraphs 3-6 in relation to the passage as a whole is to:

   F. shift the passage's focus toward the FDA's lack of concern for American citizens.
   G. reinforce the passage's claim that contaminants are allowed to exist in food.
   H. satirically comment on the FDA's established guidelines for levels of food contaminants.
   J. provide information from the FDA about the foods with the most contaminants.

19. It can reasonably be inferred that the line "So, the next time you have a fly in your soup, don't be so quick to blame the chef!" (lines 91-92) most closely means which of the following?

   A. Don't be so quick to judge the restaurant for the additional protein a fly provides.
   B. Be sure to have proof of a fly in your soup before sending it back to the kitchen.
   C. A fly could have gotten into the soup at the numerous locations handling the ingredients.
   D. Be certain your food is clear of contaminants before eating.

20. The author's use of sentences like "Thank you, FDA!" (line 49) and "Sure, that's fine!" (lines 52-53), adds what kind of tone to the passage?

   F. Ironic
   G. Idealistic
   H. Malevolent
   J. Eloquent

Competitive eating is a sport in which participants compete against each other in timed events to consume large amounts of food. Once an event that largely took place at county fairs, the relatively recent media coverage of the annual Nathan's Hot Dog Eating Contest has taken this sport to a new level of exposure. The International Federation of Competitive Eating (IFOCE), which first established competitive eating as a sport in the 1990s, hosts approximately 80 "Major League Eating" events across the globe annually, giving away almost $400,000 to winners and participants. Any attempt to walk away with a handful of cash by a random bystander, though, would likely be thwarted by the trained professionals who travel far and wide to partake in such challenges.

No serious challenger could possibly compete with the eating "heavyweights" without training and knowledge of the rules. In order to gorge with little time for a breath, serious contestants train for weeks to months in advance by increasing stomach capacity. In order to do this, trainees generally drink large amounts of water in a short period of time or consume large quantities of fruits and vegetables. Consistently training with the food that is used in the competition would likely be unhealthy, especially if it were a food like hot dogs or chicken wings. During this training, the seasoned chewer will likely work on eating techniques at the same time. Some participants will dunk the food into water in order to moisten the food so it slides down the throat easier. Some incorporate a kind of jumping up and down called the "Carlene Pop" to force the food down into the stomach. Others incorporate a style called "chipmunking" in which the eater shoves as much food into the mouth as possible in the last few seconds that will count toward the total consumed if eaten in a reasonable amount of time after the final buzzer. Most eaters, however, incorporate these techniques while shoving food down the throat with very little chewing—it's practically inhaling.

Throughout the actual contest, a minor amount of food debris is allowed, but if the competitor cannot hold the amount of food filling the stomach, a "reversal" is called and the contestant is disqualified. For Takeru Kobayashi, six-time winner of the Nathan's Hot Dog Eating Contest, this apparent fault became a reality in 2007 after eating 63 hot dogs in 12 minutes, though the IFOCE sided with Kobayashi. Still, Kobayashi fell to the winner, Joey Chestnut, who ingested 66 hot dogs; he remains the record holder and retained the prized "Mustard Yellow Belt" for eight consecutive years by winning the Coney Island competition until losing in 2015 to Matt Stonie.

The two eating powerhouses have arguably brought competitive eating to a higher level of popularity. Kobayashi and Chestnut have gone at it multiple times since 2005 at the Nathan's Contest, but Kobayashi has been impressing audiences since 2001. Before Kobayashi's 2001 performance of 50 hot dogs and buns in 12 minutes (an average of more than 4 dogs and buns a minute!), crowds were used to seeing eaters chow down on 20-25 in the same amount of time. Kobayashi doubled the world record and put the crowd in a frenzy! Never before had a competitor gorged himself in the way Kobayashi did. In 2004, ESPN exposed the contest to the world, and viewers were stunned to see the skill in which the Japanese eater established a new world record of 53 and one half dogs and buns. The following year, Chestnut's debut at Coney Island, Kobayashi continued to dominate and took in 49 and handed Chestnut a distant third place; only 32 dogs were downed in his first year. 2006 featured two new records: the world record claimed by Kobayashi (54) and the U.S. record by Chestnut (52) as he inched closer to dethroning Kobayashi.

In the 2007 contest, Chestnut targeted gold, or, more appropriately, mustard yellow. Kobayashi fell for the first time in six years and added insult to injury when he apparently fouled in the last minute. Chestnut took the Mustard that year, but the following year pitted this pair against each other once again to end in a tie in the new 10 minute time limit. Chestnut finished his overtime plate of five dogs just before Kobayashi and took hold of the belt once again. Chestnut has gone on to stretch the world record to 69 hot dogs but without his nemesis and competitive eating pioneer by his side. Kobayashi has not participated since 2009, citing a contract dispute, but the world waits for his return and a classic Kobayashi-Chestnut matchup.

From pickles to peanut butter and banana sandwiches to the American staple, the hot dog, competitive eaters take on any challenge and travel the world to do it. Though the most widely known competition is held in Coney Island, competitions exist at all times and locations—your own state fair or favorite restaurant might just have an eating competition. Whether one finds it disgusting or impressive, competitive eating is a sport enjoyed by many and likely shunned by many more. Since July 4th is our nation's Independence Day, can it be said that the hot dog is as American as apple pie? (By the way, apple pie eating contests are held at state fairs across the country).

84

21. It can reasonably be inferred from the passage that competitors train by eating fruits and vegetables (lines 22-23) because:

A. the fibrous material expands in the stomach.
B. many competitors live a vegetarian lifestyle outside the competition.
C. they are low calorie options for eating in such large quantities.
D. competitors are always concerned about physically being out of shape.

22. According to the author, which of the following is NOT likely a reason why competitive eating has gained popularity?

F. ESPN's coverage of the Nathan's Hot Dog Eating Contest
G. Takeru Kobayashi's 2007 suspected fault
H. Takeru Kobayashi and Joey Chestnut's close competitions
J. Joey Chestnut's recent performances

23. The primary purpose of the passage is to:

A. inform readers of the training regiments required for competitive eating.
B. persuade readers to avoid the crowd at Coney Island on July 4th.
C. inform readers of a sport growing in popularity.
D. persuade readers to try out local eating competitions.

24. According to the passage, the "Mustard Yellow Belt" is attained by:

F. achieving victory at any competitive eating competition.
G. breaking the world record for hot dogs consumed at Nathan's Hot Dog Eating Contest.
H. winning the Nathan's Hot Dog Eating Contest for nine years in a row.
J. eating the most hot dogs at an annual Nathan's Hot Dog Eating Contest.

25. It can reasonably be inferred that a *reversal* as used in line 41 means:

A. judges' disqualification.
B. regurgitation.
C. the contestant turning his back to the judges.
D. refusal to finish eating.

26. The line "competitive eating is a sport enjoyed by many and likely shunned by many more" (line 93-94) indicates the author's:

F. passion for the sport of competitive eating.
G. presumption that the reader may not appreciate the sport.
H. personal experience watching crowds gasp and turn in disgust during competitions.
J. exclusionist attitude to those who do not enjoy competitive eating contests.

27. The author provides competitive eating techniques like the "Carlene Pop" (line 30) and "chipmunking" (line 32) in order to provide:

A. a brief history of where the sport has been and where it is headed.
B. respect for those who can perform such methods.
C. background information for the reader to understand competitive eaters do more than just chew fast.
D. methods the professionals use only when practicing.

28. In chronological order, the following events happened in what sequence?
   I. Kobayashi doubles a world record.
   II. Chestnut wins his first "Mustard Yellow Belt."
   III. Chestnut and Kobayashi take their contest into overtime.

F. I, II, III
G. I, III, II
H. II, I, III
J. III, II, I

29. The author includes the line "(By the way, apple pie eating contests are held at state fairs across the country)" (lines 96-97) in order to:
A. suggest that the sport of competitive eating is prevalent.
B. convince the reader to attend a competition.
C. suggest apple pie is one of America's favorite foods.
D. inspire those with a sweet tooth to seek out apple pie.

30. It can reasonably be inferred that the author believes competitive eating first amazed large audiences in:

F. the 1990s.
G. 2001.
H. 2004.
J. 2007.

Physically, we cannot change much about who we are. Certainly gaining and losing weight or packing on muscle can alter our appearances, but most of how we look is based on our genes. Though modern science is
5 beginning to meddle with the human genetic code in order to identify and manipulate certain genes, there is no need for a genetic scientist's interference when attempting to determine the natural heredity of some common human features. Nearly all physical traits are inherited through
10 the genes of one's parents; a widow's peak, attached earlobes, and a rolling tongue are common traits studied in science classes. Eye color, and more specifically, how one ends up with a certain eye color, seems to be the trait that interests students most. When people strongly desire a
15 certain trait to be passed down to their children, they can simply search for the complementary traits in a mate, or, as science improves, may simply call up the doctor for an eye color change.

Why do we have the eye colors we do? One only
20 has to look at his or her own genetics to arrive at the reason for eye color. Melanin, or dark pigment (also responsible for hair and skin color), is what is present in the eye that determines eye color, and more specifically, the amount of melanin in the iris. Brown eyes reflect a
25 heavy amount of the pigment, whereas green and blue eyes have significantly less melanin. Three genes have thus far been determined by scientists as those responsible for eye color, and, of course, these genes are inherited from one's parents. Genes from parents sketch out a
30 "body road map," including eye color and practically everything else for children. Children inherit one copy of a gene from their mothers and one from their fathers. Looking at children's parents, therefore, will help determine the likelihood of a certain eye color. The combination of
35 genes for a given trait is called the genotype, whereas the appearance of the genes is called the phenotype.

An entertaining activity for a student of basic biology is to determine the likelihood of a certain eye color for his or her future children with a possible mate.
40 First, one should learn the eye colors of both the mate and both pairs of parents. By examining inheritance, the potential phenotypes are revealed. When working with eye color inheritance, though, it is important to know that brown eyes are dominant while blue eyes are recessive.
45 This means that in the realm of possibilities, a brown eye gene will essentially "override" a blue eye gene when put in combination. For example, if a blue-eyed female and brown-eyed male, each with parents showing the same phenotype as their children, had a child together, the like-
50 lihood of a brown-eyed child would be about 75%. A

child in this simple scenario would have a 25% chance to have something other than brown eyes (green or blue). This is because the dominant brown eye gene masks the recessive blue eye gene in 50% of the possibilities. In
55 more complex situations, in order to discover all the potential combinations of genotypes, a small chart called a Punnett Square is typically used because genetic possibilities can vary greatly.

Although studying genetic possibilities can help
60 predict future children's traits, it does little for the eye color one already has. In fact, many teens and adults focus on eye color as a characteristic they can change since it takes little effort. Since the mid-eighties, color contacts have been available to those who wanted a quick, easy,
65 and painless physical change, but now a permanent solution for changing brown eyes to blue is in the works. One California doctor says that he has developed a process to laser away the brown pigment to leave the underlying blue. Though this is still being studied, other doctors have
70 doubts about the procedure's safety. Some claim that the destruction of melanin would leave behind remnants similar to the ashes left behind from a burned log. This may lead to future issues with cataracts, or worse, glaucoma, a serious eye condition that can lead to permanent vision
75 loss. With an expected price tag of $5,000, are the combined price and risk worth altering what nature created?

The genes inherited from our parents determine essentially everything about an individual, and methods for predicting future generations' traits can be used. Our
80 own eye color, determined by the amount of melanin in our irises, is truly the result of our parents' genotypes. However, as technology continues to change our physical traits, can altering our eye color eventually lead to our vision of the future becoming dark?

31. The passage indicates that a genotype is:

   A. the genetic makeup of a trait.
   B. the bodily manifestation of a trait.
   C. the gene required to produce a certain trait.
   D. a parent's chosen trait for a child.

32. The primary purpose of the passage is to:

   F. describe the process by which students can determine the eye color of their future offspring.
   G. inform readers of simple genetics and options available to alter some inherited traits.
   H. inform readers of scientific breakthroughs.
   J. persuade readers to rethink surgery altering physical features.

33. It is reasonable to conclude that the author ends the fourth paragraph with the question, "Are the combined price and risk worth altering what nature created?" (lines 75-76) in order to:

A. make the reader think about the choice he or she is about to make.
B. state that natural characteristics should not be altered.
C. suggest that the risk involved does not justify such a minor cosmetic change.
D. suggest that a medical procedure involving important parts of one's body should not be attempted.

34. The author identifies all of the following as ways to modify one's appearance EXCEPT:

F. medical procedure.
G. working out.
H. wearing color contact lenses.
J. adding melanin to one's eyes.

35. The passage indicates that a recessive gene:

A. will always be hidden unless there is a dominant trait.
B. can remain physically unseen in a brown-eyed individual.
C. may change the eye color of an individual over time.
D. has a 25% chance to be evident in all circumstances.

36. The central argument doctors have against permanently changing eye color is:

F. the doctor from California doesn't use lasers as intended.
G. scar tissue may seriously damage vision.
H. cataracts form from eye procedures involving lasers.
J. the cost of such a procedure would be too expensive for how simple a process it is.

37. It can reasonably be inferred from information in the passage that one would find a Punnett Square to be most helpful in which of the following circumstances?

A. When attempting to determine what color eyes a child will have if one parent has brown eyes and the other has green eyes
B. When attempting to determine what color eyes a child will have if one parent has blue eyes and the eye color of the other parent is unknown
C. When wishing to determine the likely eye color of a child when both parents have brown eyes
D. When determining what gender a child will be

38. It can be reasonably inferred from the passage that the less melanin one has in his or her skin:

F. the lighter a bruise on the skin will be.
G. the lighter the eye color will be.
H. the tanner one will get when exposed to the sun.
J. the lighter his or her skin will be.

39. Which of the following statements best describes the way the second paragraph functions in the passage as a whole?

A. It provides information required to understand the function and purpose of a Punnett Square.
B. It divides the passage into two parts, one focused on heredity, the other on surgical methods.
C. It provides basic information about genetics that is required to understand the sources of eye color.
D. It functions as a transition between the first paragraph and the author's personal feelings about altering genetics.

40. Which of the following is NOT a phenotype inherited from one's parents?

F. brain damage
G. hair color
H. toe length
J. teeth straightness

ANSWER KEYS, SKILLS, & EXPLANATIONS

ANSWER	SKILL(S)	EXPLANATION
1. B	WORD CHOICE	*But also* in choice B suggests the addition of a similar detail, which does NOT reflect a contrast in ideas.
2. F	ADDING, REVISING, AND DELETING INFORMATION	The underlined portion elaborates upon the previously stated idea that Lady Gaga's music career "started much earlier." It provides specific details about how long Lady Gaga has been involved with music, making choice F the best answer.
3. C	WORDINESS AND REDUNDANCY	The word *solo* means "on one's own," making choice A redundant. Likewise, choice B is redundant because *unaccompanied* means "by oneself," and choice D is repetitive because *autonomous* means "alone." Thus, choice C is the only option that is not redundant and overly wordy.
4. J	RUN-ON SENTENCES	Choice F creates a run-on sentence because it fuses together two complete thoughts. Choice G contains a conjunction, but lacks the necessary comma that should accompany a conjunction that is used to join two complete thoughts. In choice H, the word *where* does not make sense, since we are not referring to a location. Choice J is the best fit because it corrects the run-on by replacing the complete thought with a fragment that adds additional information to the complete thought.
5. C	VERB TENSE	Choices A, B, and D all provide an appropriate verb tense to describe Akon's role in Gaga's career. Choice C, *becoming*, is flawed, though, because it is lacking a helping verb. Since this is a NOT question, choice C, the choice that does not fit in the passage, should be the answer.
6. H	ORGANIZATION	We need to figure out what word in the sentence the modifier, "a moniker inspired by the Queen song 'Radio Ga Ga,'" is intended to describe. A moniker is a nickname—Stephanie Germonatta's nickname is "Lady Gaga," which appears at the end of the sentence. By selecting choice H, we place the underlined portion immediately after the stage name it was intended to describe.
7. B	COMMAS	The title of the album, *The Fame*, is what is known as a nonessential appositive: a noun that renames another noun in the sentence, but does not need to be there in order for the sentence to make sense. An artist can only have one debut album; therefore, the title of the album is not necessary to know which album we are referring to. Nonessential elements should be offset from the rest of the sentence with commas. Although choice D would be more concise, in this example the album's title is relevant, though still a nonessential appositive, as the sentence goes on to say that it "lived up to its name." Choice C should not be chosen because it is wordy.
8. J	SENTENCE FRAGMENTS	The present participial *climbing* does not have a helping verb, which means that the underlined portion is missing a predicate and is not a complete sentence. The revision with the past tense verb *climbed* (choice J) eliminates this issue and creates a complete sentence.
9. A	WORD CHOICE	The function of this paragraph is to provide another example of Lady Gaga's mass appeal. Choice A, *In addition to*, signals that more details and examples follow, making it the best choice. While choice D, *plus*, is also an addition word, it creates a fragment. Choices B and C should be eliminated because they change the meaning of the topic sentence.
10. F	PRONOUNS AND VERB TENSE	First, we need to decide whether to use the pronoun *who* or *whom*. *Designers, stylists, and artists* are the subject of the clause, so we can eliminate the object pronoun *whom* (choices G and J). Next, we need to decide which verb choice to select from the remaining options. The paragraph is comprised of simple present tense verbs (*captivates*, *is*, *explains*, *sees*), so the simple present tense verb *work* in choice F makes it the best option.

ANSWER KEY AND EXPLANATIONS

11. D	**SENTENCE STRUCTURE**	Since this is a NOT question, let's use the process of elimination. Choice A is grammatically correct because it uses the conjunction *because* to link the two complete thoughts. Choice B would work because it uses a semicolon to join the two complete thoughts. Choice C is appropriate because it uses the conjunction *since* to show the relationship between the two ideas. Therefore, choice D is our answer choice because it contains a mistake: It creates a run-on sentence by omitting a necessary semicolon between the words *package* and *although*.
12. J	**WORDINESS**	Choice J is the most concise while also being grammatically correct and maintaining the intended meaning of the sentence.
13. C	**ORGANIZATION**	Option C would create a split infinitive, which incorrectly separates a helping verb from a main verb. Since this is an EXCEPT question, we should choose the option that contains an error.
14. G	**ORGANIZATION**	First, decide on the best topic sentence for this paragraph. This paragraph is about Gaga's message of self-expression and individuality, which is established in sentence 2. Once you have decided to begin the paragraph with sentence 2, go ahead and eliminate choices F and H. Now, decide which sentence should be second, sentence 4 (choice G) or sentence 1 (choice J). Sentence 4 would be next because it counters the idea in sentence 2. From there, sentence 3 begins with the introductory phrase "despite this criticism," which is a reference to the idea presented in sentence 4. The paragraph would end with sentence 1, which refers to her avoidance of the "sophomore slump" that is mentioned at the end of sentence 3.
15. B	**ADDING, DELETING, AND REVISING INFORMATION**	First, use the process of elimination to narrow down your choices—since the passage ends by saying that Gaga is "breaking the mold for generations of performers to come," we can say that YES, the statement should be added (so eliminate choices C and D). Now, we need to decide WHY the statement should be added. The author's purpose is not to discuss Ke$ha and Nicki Minaj's popularity (choice A), but rather to emphasize the ongoing impact Lady Gaga has on the music industry (choice B).

ANSWER	SKILL(S)	EXPLANATION
16. H	SENTENCE FRAGMENTS	The conjunction *while* makes the first half of the underlined portion a sentence fragment. To fix it, combine the dependent clause to the independent clause that follows it, using a comma to link the two (choice H).
17. B	ADDING, DELETING, AND REVISING INFORMATION	The parentheses around this statement indicate that it is an aside, providing information that is slightly off-topic. Due to the parentheses, then, we can decide to keep the statement, which eliminates choices C and D. Now we need to decide what purpose this information serves in the passage. Since the previous sentence labels Hilton as a hypocrite, choice B is the best option.
18. F	SENTENCE STRUCTURE/ADJECTIVES AND ADVERBS	The ACT English test favors a very simple, straightforward sentence structure: First the subject, then the verb, then any objects or modifiers. The subject is Hilton, so eliminate choices G and H. Now consider the modifier *bad* (choice F) or *badly* (choice J). We aren't describing how the example *served* (choice J), but rather what kind of *example* it was (choice F). Therefore, choose the adjective *bad* to describe the noun *example*, which makes choice F the correct answer.
19. A	WORD CHOICE	The present tense verbs in this paragraph indicate that the author is discussing Perez Hilton's current career, which is best supported with the transition word *nowadays* (choice A).
20. G	WORDINESS AND REDUNDANCY	Choice F can be eliminated because *pressure* and *strain* mean something similar. Choices H and J and unnecessarily wordy and slightly change the intended meaning. Therefore, choice G is the best option.
21. A	PUNCTUATION	The first half of the sentence serves as an introductory phrase. When a prepositional phrase or dependent clause appears before a complete thought, offset it with a comma (choice A).
22. J	WORD CHOICE	Choices F and G can be eliminated because they incorrectly use an adjective when we would need an adverb to modify the verb *helped*. The phrase "somewhat on accident" should be offset by commas, and even then, it would create a split infinitive between the helping verb *have* and the main verb *helped*. Therefore, eliminate the underlined portion (choice J).
23. B	PRONOUNS / VERB TENSE	Choice B incorrectly uses the object pronoun *whom*. Since this is an EXCEPT question, the option that contains a mistake is our answer.
24. J	WORD CHOICE	We need to eliminate the three options that would correctly show a cause-effect relationship between these two ideas. Those options would be choices F, G, and H. Choice J, *despite*, changes the meaning by introducing a contrast; since this is a NOT question, choice J is the answer.
25. C	SENTENCE STRUCTURE / WORDINESS	Aim to maintain parallel structure here. We are listing three entities—option C is written best because it presents three single-word nouns. It is the most straight-forward and concise.
26. G	ORGANIZATION	Choice F can be eliminated because Hilton was not a struggling actor overnight. Get rid of choice H because it separates a verb from its object. Choice J doesn't work because it separates the modifier "of a successful website" from the noun it describes. Thus, G is the answer.
27. B	ADDING, DELETING, AND REVISING INFORMATION	The beginning of the sentence tells us that "*PerezHilton.com* gained attention for" something. If the underlined portion were removed, it would be unclear to the reader what about his celebrity photos garnered so much attention (choice B).
28. H	WORD CHOICE	The structure of the question indicates that the original word choice in the passage,

ANSWER KEY AND EXPLANATIONS

...

		surpassed, IS acceptable. Since this is a NOT question, eliminate the three answer choices that are most similar in meaning to *surpassed* (choices F, G, and J), and select the answer choice that is most different in meaning (*amplified*, choice H).
29. A	**PRONOUNS**	We know that will.i.am confronted Hilton. An individual usually confronts someone about that person's behavior, not his or her own. Thus, we can eliminate choice B. Choice C can be eliminated because "Black Eyed Peas" is plural, but the pronoun *his* is singular. Choice D can be eliminated because Fergie is a woman, but *his* is a masculine pronoun. We also know that choice A is correct because the paragraph goes on to say that "Perez responded." That indicates that Perez Hilton was responding to his own behavior that will.i.am. took issue with.
30. H	**ORGANIZATION**	Begin by deciding which paragraph would make the best introduction. Paragraph 3 begins broadly, then narrows its focus to introducing a specific individual. Thus, eliminate choices F and G. Now, decide which paragraph should be second: paragraph 4 (choice H) or paragraph J (choice J). Paragraph 3 ends by discussing the crude pictures Hilton drew. The beginning of paragraph 4, "Such negativity," is a reference to the idea presented at the end of paragraph 3. That makes paragraph 4 the next logical paragraph. Paragraph 1 would be next, as "this incident" is a reference to the altercation between Hilton and will.i.am described at the end of paragraph 3. Finally, paragraph 2 describes the outcome of Hilton's realization that was mentioned at the end of paragraph 1.

	ANSWER	SKILL(S)	EXPLANATION
ANSWER KEY AND EXPLANATIONS	31. A	ADDING INFORMATION	The detailed statement provides examples of status symbols and "designer duds," thus providing additional support for the opening sentence.
	32. G	VERB TENSE	The passage discusses a current, ongoing phenomenon, which would make the present progressive tense "is gaining" the most appropriate. Notice the clue in the following sentence: "are choosing." Maintain consistent verb tenses throughout the paragraph.
	33. A	WORD CHOICE	The conjunction *and* joins the two equal examples to one another. All of the other possible choices would change the meaning of the sentence by adding in an unnecessary contrast between ideas.
	34. J	PUNCTUATION	Beginning with the word *while*, the first half of this sentence is a dependent clause (an incomplete thought). When a dependent clause appears before an independent clause, separate both clauses with a comma.
	35. C	PUNCTUATION	The phrase "the world's most expensive dog" is a nonessential appositive; in other words, it is a phrase that renames or restates the noun Big Splash. The phrase gives a nonessential, additional piece of information about Big Splash; therefore, offset it with a comma.
	36. H	VERB TENSE	Replace the underlined portion with the present tense verb *is* to maintain consistent present tense with the other verbs (*prefer, is,* and *comes*).
	37. C	MISPLACED MODIFIERS	The phrase "marked by his fiery red fur" is intended to describe the dog Big Splash, so it should be placed near his name.
	38. H	PUNCTUATION	We often see a semicolon before the word *however*. In this case, though, a comma is the best choice. Why? In this sentence, the word *however* is not being used to join two complete thoughts (in which case we would use a semicolon before it and a comma after it), but rather it is serving as an interruption or aside from single complete thought expressed in the sentence. Therefore, use a comma before and after the word *however* to offset this interruption.
	39. A	ADJECTIVES	*Unusual* and *unique* describe different attributes of designer dog species. The word *peculiar* in choices B and C slightly change the meaning, implying something strange. The comparative *more* in choice D is unnecessary since the word *unique* means, "one of a kind." Something cannot be more one of a kind than another. This is an example of an absolute modifier—words like *unique* and *perfect* should not be used with comparative or superlative words (more, most).
	40. H	VERB CHOICE	Eliminate choice F because it creates a run-on sentence and choice J because it creates a fragment. Choice G is too wordy, and there should be a comma before the word *which*. Therefore, choice H is the best option.
	41. A	WORD CHOICE	The phrase "seek out" is the best complement to the phrase "those looking for," as *seek* and "look for" are synonyms. The other choices change the meaning and have a different connotation.
	42. F	ADDING INFORMATION	The example about Jessica Simpson and her dog helps the author illustrate the point made in the paragraph's topic sentence.
	43. D	PRONOUNS	The antecedent for the pronoun is the plural noun *pups*, and we are discussing the style of those dogs, so the plural possessive *their* is the best choice.
	44. G	MISPLACED MODIFIERS	Placing the modifier after the word *promote* would lead to confusion in meaning. Therefore, it is the only choice that is not acceptable.
	45. A	WORD CHOICE	The word *therefore* is the most fitting for the conclusion of the passage by showing the connection between the earlier examples and the author's final point, while also maintain the style and tone of the passage as a whole.

ANSWER	SKILL(S)	EXPLANATION
46. H	SENTENCE STRUCTURE	In order to maintain parallel structure with the verb *throwing*, use the similarly-structured verb *rummaging*. Be sure to include the conjunction *and* to link both phrases.
47. B	VERB TENSE	The paragraph describes the ongoing process of Lucy trying to wean herself off of sugar. Therefore, the progressive verb *was proving* shows this action that was ongoing in the past.
48. J	ADDING OR DELETING INFORMATION	The passage describes how difficult it was for Lucy to kick her sugar habit. The underlined portion provides additional details that illustrate that struggle.
49. A	SENTENCE STRUCTURE	Choices B and C are wrong because they would create a run-on sentence. Choice D changes the intended meaning of the sentence. Choice A, therefore, is the best option, because it serves as an introductory phrase that describes Lucy and her addiction to sugar.
50. F	REVISING INFORMATION	The key phrase in the question is "ingrained quality." In other words, the writer wants to show that Lucy naturally has a sweet tooth. Choice F implies this idea by suggesting that Lucy was drawn to a job at a candy shop because of her strong inclination towards sweets.
51. C	WORD CHOICE	The word *despite* shows the contrast between Lucy's unhealthy eating habits and her healthy weight.
52. H	WORD CHOICE	The word *however* illustrates how, although her weight was within the healthy range, Lucy realized that her poor nutrition would likely have an adverse effect on her health one day.
53. B	PRONOUNS & VERBS	Use the subject pronoun *who* to serve as the subject of the phrase, and the past tense verb *knew* to maintain consistent past tense with the rest of the passage.
54. J	VERB TENSE	Choice F is wrong because it uses the noun *effects* instead of the verb *affects*. Choice G is incorrect because it incorrectly uses the expression *would of* instead of *would have*. Choice H, similar to choice F, also mixes us *effect* and *affect*.
55. C	MISPLACED MODIFIERS	The underlined portion is intended to describe Lucy, so the best placement is right by her name.
56. G	WORD CHOICE	*Of course, clearly,* and *undoubtedly* are the most similar in meaning to the underlined word, *obviously*. The word *frankly*, though, means, "in a truthful, direct way."
57. D	SENTENCE STRUCTURE	Use a comma after *pantry* to offset the dependent clause (incomplete thought) from the independent clause (complete thought) that follows it.
58. F	ADDING OR DELETING INFORMATION	The suggested portion should be added because it explains Lucy's difficulty with avoiding all forms of sugar by elaborating on the extent to which sugar is present in unexpected foods.
59. C	WORD CHOICE	The phrase "after dinner" indicates a period of time, which is best conveyed by the word *when*.
60. F	PUNCTUATION	Although colons introduce lists, choice F does not fit because it does not include any kind of punctuation to transition from the end of the list to the remainder of the sentence. By contrast, notice how choices G, H, and J all include punctuation that offsets both the beginning and the end of the list.

ANSWER KEY AND EXPLANATIONS

ANSWER	SKILL(S)	EXPLANATION
61. B	WORD CHOICE	Choice B, *perps*, which is short for *perpetrators*, is a slang term. Slang should be avoided on the ACT.
62. H	WORDINESS & REDUNDANCY	The underlined portion (choice F) and choice J are both redundant. Choice G makes the sentence awkward and the meaning unclear. Therefore, H is the best option.
63. C	WORD CHOICE	While the word *stereotypical* can also have a negative connotation, it is not as strong as the other three choices. Also, the sentence is intended to describe the laws themselves. The laws are not stereotypical (though some may argue that they reinforce negative stereotypes).
64. F	SENTENCE STRUCTURE	Choices H and J should be eliminated because they sound like teens and young adults in general, not the sagging pants they wear, are featured in music videos. Choice F is a better option because it includes the phrase *more recently,* which serves a transition from the previous sentence, which mentions the earlier decade of the 1990s.
65. D	PUNCTUATION	The word *though* serves as an interruption from the main clause of the sentence, so it should be offset on both sides with commas (choice D).
66. F	MISPLACED MODIFIER	The placement of the underlined portion correctly provides an explanation for the claim established in the first part of the sentence.
67. C	WORDINESS & REDUNDANCY	*Creative* and *ingenious* are similar in meaning (choice A), as are *artistic* and *inventive* (choice B); these should be eliminated. Choice D changes the intended meaning of the passage, leaving C as the best answer.
68. J	SENTENCE STRUCTURE	Choices F, G, and H are unclear in meaning: What (or who) is being "displayed on a bulletin board"? Choice J provides clarification with the addition of the subject *pictures*.
69. A	ADDING & DELETING INFORMATION	Without the underlined portion, many readers would be left scratching their heads as to the meaning and origin of the term *Urkeled*. Therefore, the clarification should be kept in order to explain this unfamiliar term to the readers and to clarify the connection between the school's actions and the terminology they used.
70. G	WORD CHOICE	On the ACT, as long as it is grammatically correct, choose the most formal, least conversational word or phrase, which in this case is "appalled by."
71. C	WORD CHOICE	The underlined portion *though* provides a hint that we want a word that conveys an exception or a contrast. The word *consequently*, suggests a cause-and-effect relationship, making it the weakest option but the correct choice in this NOT question.
72. G	WORD CHOICE	The sentence is showing a contrast between displaying basketball shorts or underwear underneath sagging pants. Expressions like *rather than* (F), *as an alternative to* (H), and *in place of* (J) highlight the two choices students have with this fashion style.
73. D	SENTENCE STRUCTURE	The sentence intends to show a connection between Larry Platt and the performance of his song. Choice A, though, creates a run-on sentence. Instead, the word *whose* (D) refers to both a person (Platt) and the performance which he possesses.
74. F	PUNCTUATION	The expression "just to play it safe" is an interruption to the main clause of the sentence, so it needs to be offset. This can be done with parentheses (choice G), dashes (choice H), or commas (choice J). This leaves choice F as the exception.
75. B	ORGANIZATION	Paragraph 1 (choices B and C) should come first, as it provides a general introduction and then outlines the topic of the passage. Paragraph 1 ends by mentioning the trend's jailhouse origins; therefore, Paragraph 4 would be next, since it begins with "this connection to criminals," a reference to the end of paragraph 1.

ANSWER	SKILL(S)	EXPLANATION
1. B	SUPPORTING DETAILS	Be careful of *EXCEPT* or *NOT* questions. Paragraph 2 mentions Justin's mom; however, he follows her advice on how to treat a girl. He clearly thinks over how courteous he was in the same paragraph (A), is concerned about his peers in lines 52-56 (C), and how the insects seem to be mocking him in paragraph 4 (D).
2. J	DRAWING CONCLUSIONS	The question's phrasing suggests main idea, but is really a drawing conclusions question—you have to determine the best choice, and it is not directly stated in the passage. J states what Justin thought after the date ended and is supported by lines 38-40.
3. D	DRAWING CONCLUSIONS	Another *EXCEPT* question. Choices B and C describe the insects and how Justin imagined that they were closely watching and responding to the events. Choice A is displayed in lines 53-56. He doesn't think about the possibility of her coming back out of the house (choice D) even though she does later. This makes choice D the exception.
4. F	DRAWING CONCLUSIONS	The question is asking about the girl here, not the entire date. Don't get confused by phrasing! There is no evidence to suggest pity (G), poor kissing (H), or prevention of rumors (J). The best option here is to choose F, that she was nervous to kiss him at her doorstep but came back to show her interest and excitement before he left in his car.
5. B	SUPPORTING DETAILS	There is really no tension between the two teenagers (A), and there is no suggestion of parents peeking in on their goodbye (C), or a concern about her breath (D). The scene is emphasized through the narrator's shared opinion of the event.
6. F	AUTHOR'S PURPOSE/ MAIN IDEA	Through the results of the night, we can assume the author thinks that nice guys don't always finish last. G can be excluded because of the narrator and Justin's excitement when the night ends, and H is too vague. J may be a possibility, but the excitement demonstrated when Justin goes to bed clearly suggests that the existence of chivalry is not the main message.
7. B	DRAWING CONCLUSIONS	When questions refer to specific lines, take a few seconds to read a sentence or two before and after the lines to get the complete idea. It seems as though Justin didn't want poppy, fun music playing while he sulked; however, he wasn't necessarily looking for a sad song (C). In fact, he addresses the radio station with frustration because of the slow, sad song lyrics that played. He was mostly interested in "abandoning the scene of his failure" (line 68), and with that, the pop music they most likely listened to on the date.
8. F	SUPPORTING DETAILS	A key testing strategy is "don't just pick a word because you don't know its meaning." In the case of the word *apathy* (J), it means "lack of interest or concern." Justin *is* quite concerned about the situation, so choice J should be eliminated. He isn't bitter or wishing to get even at the girl for what she did, so the word *spite* (G) isn't correct either. He also questions what went wrong in line 1, so he clearly doesn't display understanding (H).
9. D	SUPPORTING DETAILS	This is a bit of a tricky question, and it is quite possible that on the real test, you will find an answer that could be placed before the true answer. Among the choices, option B refers to lines 30-32, but under closer review, it refers to teachers, as in *all* teachers in general, yelling at students. They are only thinking about one, Mrs. Shulter. You cannot generalize about the rest of the teachers. Option C, again, presents a similar problem. Recall that Justin is only *imagining* the kids making fun—this isn't reality. Option D is the only absolutely true option. Line 30 states, "*their* junior English teacher."
10. H	AUTHOR'S PURPOSE	Think like the author here and combine Justin's opinion about the situation, too. Look back at the entire situation starting on line 33 and ending on line 40. Though his imagined "movie girl" cuddles up, she doesn't necessarily anticipate and want such an action from a guy (F)—movies are made up! Justin knows of such a move, but doesn't do so to try to be respectful (G). This is also not likely considered to be "inappropriate behavior" (J), so contrasting Justin and his hesitant yet respectful behavior with the fictional suave guy is the best choice.

ANSWER KEY AND EXPLANATIONS

ANSWER	SKILL(S)	EXPLANATION
11. A	MAIN IDEA	The transition from the previous paragraph (lines 35-36) may have led you to believe that option A was established in the paragraph, but this was only leading to what is further discussed in the next two paragraphs. Since this is an *EXCEPT* question, option A should be selected.
12. G	SUPPORTING DETAILS	Option G is suggested throughout paragraph 1. Choice F features an absolute statement in "the restaurant <u>always</u> pleases…" These absolutes can try to hide in your answers. If choosing an answer like choice F, you better be sure you can find support that it <u>always</u> happens. Choice H makes a claim that seasonal items are highly sought out when released. They may be popular, but you'd need proof to say that they are "highly sought." Besides, McRib isn't even mentioned in the passage. Choice J, again, uses one of those absolute statements; McDonald's will not force anyone to eat something!
13. B	SUPPORTING DETAILS	Paragraph 5 (lines 65-75) should be your target to answer this Indian McDonald's question. Lines 65-66 state that the Maharaja Mac consists of two chicken patties, and chicken is considered meat. Option D may have tripped up some test takers, but the essential information is provided in the parentheses—*aloo* means *potato* (lines 67-68).
14. J	DRAWING CONCLUSIONS	Lines 6-11 focus on McDonald's customers' desires for salads and fruit. These lines provide examples to highlight its willingness to provide customers with healthier options and meet their demands.
15. A	DRAWING CONCLUSIONS	Options B, C, and D all are absolute statements, and the reader should be cautious of statements like these. "<u>Will</u> enjoy" (B), "vegetables <u>are</u> eaten" (C), and "<u>do not</u> appeal" (D) declare that the entire statement MUST be true. Certainly, this cannot be proven. Option A is most logical, and even if you have not eaten a veggie burger, changes are other Americans have eaten them.
16. F	AUTHOR'S PURPOSE	By detailing menu items from around the world, we can infer that the intended audience would not know of these foods. The passage is not intended for international travelers who wish to plan out food options on a trip simply because the passage is extremely broad in focus and discusses many different menus from around the world (H). After all, what international traveler would plan a trip based what McDonald's is offering in that country?
17. C	DRAWING CONCLUSIONS	"North of the American border" in line 51 and "provinces" (line 52) suggest Canada. Yes, you may need a bit of geographical knowledge to answer this question, but there these hints should lead you to option C.
18. H	MAIN IDEA	When dealing with a main idea question, ask yourself, "What is this passage or paragraph mostly about?" Option H suggests that regional American menu items are still familiar foods to the people in the area. The other options don't match the major idea of the paragraph. People aren't focused on preserving their favorite foods (F), option G is more of an opinion, and option J deals with McDonald's roots, which is not discussed.
19. C	DRAWING CONCLUSIONS	Seeing a familiar sight like a McDonald's in a foreign country may bring a sense of home, but the menu itself may be vastly different. Option C solidifies this idea. Nowhere in the passage does it suggest the golden arches looks different (A), and the statement isn't about a traveler's plans (B). Nor is the line suggestive of a "culture shock" for those who are not prepared for difference (D).
20. F	SUPPORTING DETAILS	A *NOT* question. Although some may have seen or even eaten McWings in an American McDonald's, we must go by what information the passage provides. Options G, H, and J can all be found in paragraph 2. McWings exist in Korean restaurants (line 48).

ANSWER KEY AND EXPLANATIONS

ANSWER	SKILL(S)	EXPLANATION
21. D	DRAWING CONCLUSIONS	"Great success" (line 15), "found large audiences" (line 19), and "had little choice but to make room for reality juggernauts" (lines 19-20) all suggest that programming changes are based on how successful programs are, which leads the reader to believe ratings are what dictate what shows will be aired.
22. J	SUPPORTING DETAILS	Lines 12-14 describe both shows in the same way within the parentheses. Perhaps a comedic jab at how the shows are essentially the same, the only difference in description is the setting (house and RV). The author doesn't mention any of the other options.
23. A	AUTHOR'S APPROACH / WORD MEANING	The words *infiltrate* and *permeate* have harsh connotations, suggesting an invasion or infestation (A) of these shows. Option B is incorrect because, based upon the ratings, the public HAS accepted these shows. Option C, though including another harsh word, *infected*, is incorrect because viewers' minds are not necessarily altered or changed from the programming changes. Finally, option D suggests a pleasurable and enlightening experience for the viewer, which clearly does not match the connotations of the words in question.
24. G	AUTHOR'S APPROACH / MAIN IDEA	Though MTV's first audience is likely unsatisfied with the removal of music from the station (F), this is not what the author wishes for readers to take away from the passage. The author is looking to create change, not simply inform that there are unhappy audiences. Options H and J also suggest that the article is meant to simply inform, but the careful reader should detect that the author's frustration adds to an argument that MTV should rethink its choices to match expectations.
25. B	AUTHOR'S APPROACH	Tone is the author's attitude toward a topic. *Ambiguous* means "uncertainty" (A)—the author's tone doesn't waver. *Refraining* means "holding back" (C), and since the author demonstrates his dissatisfaction, this is not a good choice. At the other extreme, *cruel* means "deliberately causing pain or anguish" (D). The author's tone isn't that harsh, either. He is somewhere in between refraining and cruel. He is most likely resentful and frustrated in his tone as is demonstrated in his language and word choice.
26. H	SUPPORTING DETAILS	Always be careful with the *NOT* questions. Option F is demonstrated when comparing line 1 to line 10. Option G is demonstrated throughout the passage—MTV purists would like to see music programming, of course! *TRL* was cancelled to accommodate more reality programming (line 25). What is not discussed is when videos are, if ever, shown on the station.
27. B	AUTHOR'S APPROACH	The line in question is really referring back to the previous paragraph that mentions music as merely secondary to the reality show. When provided lines, be sure to take the time to look a few lines before and after to clarify what is truly being discussed.
28. F	SEQUENCE	Sequence questions will likely never be in the proper order in the passage. You will have to use the years and timelines provided to put things in order. In this passage, however, the order is sequential. Paragraph 4 provides the reader with the order of the criticism of MTV's focus on visuals and then The Dead Kennedys release of their song after. Line 60 tells us that the logo was changed in 2010.
29. D	WORD MEANING	*Vilify* means "to make malicious and abusive statements." In the context of the lines, MTV seems to be trying to please certain viewers, not belittle them.
30. G	AUTHOR'S APPROACH	The author is obviously not a fan of the switch from music to reality programming. He would agree that these reality shows, though popular, do not have the substance and significance of the music programming that started the station (G). The author would prefer a shift back to music for the station, not taking it off the air. Line 50-54 discuss a band's song title and criticism, not his own opinions (F). Option H demonstrates another absolute statement—certainly audiences do not only care about reality shows. Though paragraph 3 mentions music credits, nowhere does it mention that these are unknown or indie artists; based on the passage, we don't know what music is played during these shows (J).

ANSWER KEY AND EXPLANATIONS

ANSWER	SKILL(S)	EXPLANATION
31. D	MAIN IDEA	The major idea presented in the passage is more about the legend and how legends can grow and change with time and public interest. Though the passage is informative, it isn't informing the reader about the Chupacabra so he or she can identify a creature (A). Option B does provide one researcher's experience; however, suggesting we do more research isn't the true purpose of the passage. Option C is more of a supporting detail only appearing in a few lines of the passage.
32. F	SUPPORTING DETAILS	*Proliferation* means "to increase in amount." The release of the book by Radford may eventually help spread the legend, but remember that the book was released as an investigation of the already popular legend. In fact, Radford tries to debunk the myth from his research.
33. C	DRAWING CONCLUSIONS	Lines 15-16 point to the beast sucking blood in the same way a vampire might. Most readers have the working background knowledge of these bloodsucking creatures, which makes option C the best choice.
34. J	DRAWING CONCLUSIONS	We cannot assume that UFO researchers take interest in <u>any unexplained</u> account (they'd be pretty busy!) (F), and there is no suggestion that the local news reported this as an alien encounter (G). Likewise, there is no evidence of UFO researchers connecting the Chupacabra with alien life. Option J is the most likely possibility.
35. A	WORD MEANING	As always, look at lines before and after the one that shows the word in question. We have hints in line 72 of what *mange* may mean: "strange jaw features and no hair." Then when we look to the line in question, we have our answer. "Facial deformities" is repeated with "strange jaw features", and "no hair" is synonymous with "mange."
36. H	DRAWING CONCLUSIONS	The final paragraph reveals Radford's thoughts that the legends are fun and that people like mysteries. This view is shared by the author—the stories and videos of these mythical creatures and others like it should only be considered entertaining, not true. Options F, G, and J all suggest some thread of truth to the tales.
37. C	SUPPORTING DETAILS	Paragraph 2 details the characteristics of the Chupacabra based on reports. Red eyes (line 22); membranous, bat-like wings (line 23); and knifelike claws (line 25) are suggested, but a protruding spinal column is not.
38. G	DRAWING CONCLUSIONS	The term "smoking gun" means "a conclusive piece of evidence." This line follows the information about Tolentino watching the movie *Species* and is referring to this revelation. The likeness of the creature and the movie's monster was evidence enough for a conclusion that Tolentino's imagination ran wild. Option F suggests that the movie was *THE REASON* for Tolentino creating the hoax, which is not true.
39. C	AUTHOR'S PURPOSE	Combine your knowledge of the passage's main purpose and the quotation marks that surround the description in line 30 to point to the fact that the author likely agrees that the Chupacabra is fictional. Choice C doesn't fit with the author's view.
40. J	DRAWING CONCLUSIONS	Lines 58-65 should lead the reader to believe that Radford thinks any Chupacabra report is simply confusion and imagination (J). Sharing a story with the local news is probably not the way someone will earn fame and fortune (F). The passage only links the film *Species* with the Chupacabra because of Tolentino, not because filmmakers used the Chupacabra myth in designing their monster (G). Radford claims that he solved the Chupacabra mystery (lines 63-64) in reference to his interviewee being confused about what she saw (lines 60-61); therefore, he would not think the beast exists in any form (H).

ANSWER	SKILL(S)	EXPLANATION
1. B	VERB TENSE	Use the present tense verb *has*, since the sentence is commenting on the current state of Facebook. Also, *has* agrees with the subject "making connections;" although *connections* ends in –*s*, the subject is actually singular, since it is the complete gerund phrase.
2. J	ADDING AND DELETING INFORMATION	The statement should be kept in the passage because the author is merely speculating on the supposed origins of the site but does not provide substantiated facts for this claim.
3. B	PUNCTUATION	Choice B creates a sentence fragment since it is missing a subject.
4. G	PRONOUN REFERENCE	The singular pronoun *it* correctly refers to the antecedent *Facebook*.
5. D	MISPLACED MODIFIER	The sentence intends to show the progress Zuckerberg made in just a few short years. If the underlined portion were moved after the word *living,* it would suggest that he lived in a dorm for a few short years, instead of the correct emphasis that his transition from being a college student to a tech giant occurred over the span of only a few years.
6. H	WORD CHOICE	Eliminate choices G and J because they use slang like "make bank" and "was an idiot." Choice F may seem better, but the expression *could have made a lot of money* is overly wordy and doesn't quite convey the profitability of the offer. Choice H is stronger because it uses slightly more sophisticated wording like *lucrative*.
7. A	ADDING AND DELETING INFORMATION	The article discusses Facebook, but then switches to a different term, "Facemash." Therefore, the explanation is necessary in order to clarify this discrepancy.
8. H	WORD CHOICE	The original choice, "according to legend," implies that the following statement may be unconfirmed. This is similar in meaning to *allegedly* (choice F), *supposedly* (choice G), and "some say" (choice J). Choice H, "without a doubt," on the other hand, means the opposite.
9. B	WORD CHOICE	"Due to" correctly emphasizes the cause and effect relationship between the first and second halves of the sentence. Choice C may sound tempting, but it slightly alters the meaning of the sentence and is overly wordy. While choice D shows the cause-and-effect relationship, it is incorrect because of the placement of the comma before the word *because*.
10. F	ADDING AND DELETING INFORMATION	The fact that Facebook originally had the article *the* in front of it is not relevant to the point made in the paragraph and, therefore, should be removed. If the paragraph's main idea were about the changes the site has gone through, then perhaps this detail would be relevant, but as it stands, it simply detracts from the paragraph's main point about the spread of Facebook around college campuses.
11. C	SENTENCE STRUCTURE	We need the word *Zuckerberg* after the verb *led* in order to clarify who is performing this action. The pronoun reference in choice B is a bit unclear, and choice D doesn't indicate that an actual individual (Zuckerberg) was responsible for the site's expansion (the site didn't just expand itself!)
12. H	WORD CHOICE	The original choice *mostly* implies that Facebook was most prevalent, but not limited to, to East Coast. Choice H, *exclusively*, means that Facebook was ONLY available on the East Coast, which is not accurate.
13. D	PUNCTUATION	The appositive phrase "twins Cameron and Tyler Winklevoss," clarifies the preceding noun *classmates*. This detail is not necessary, though, for the sentence to make sense; therefore, it should be offset with commas.

101

14. F	**WORD CHOICE/ PUNCTUATION**	*Its* (without an apostrophe) is a possessive pronoun. Ownership is not being shown in the sentence, so choices G and H should be eliminated. Choice J is incorrect because the expression should be "who would *have* thought," NOT "who would *of* thought." Choice F is correct because *it's* means, "<u>It is</u> hard to believe," which fits in the sentence.	
15. B	**SENTENCE STRUCTURE**	Choice B uses parallel structure by listing three nouns—"genius, devotion, and interest." The other choices do not demonstrate parallel structure.	

ANSWER	SKILL(S)	EXPLANATION
16. J	PRONOUN REFERENCE	Select the plural pronoun *they're* to agree with the plural antecedent *freebies*.
17. B	SENTENCE STRUCTURE	Choice A should be eliminated because it contains a sentence fragment. Choice C is incorrect because it does not contain a comma before the conjunction *and* (remember, when joining two complete thoughts with a conjunction, include a comma). Choice D is incorrect because of the semicolon—remember, semicolons should only be used to join two complete thoughts (the portion of the sentence before the semicolon in choice D is not a complete thought).
18. F	SUBJECT-VERB AGREEMENT	Be careful, here—the subject is NOT the plural noun *tours* that immediately precedes the verb, but is rather the singular noun *visit*. Choice F is the only verb that agrees with the singular subject.
19. C	VERB TENSE	The simple present tense verb *rummage* is most consistent with the other simple present tense verbs in the paragraph. Choice A is incorrect because it does not contain a helping verb (like *are*) before the present participle *looking*. Choices B and D might sound okay in the passage, but notice that their tense is not consistent with the rest of the passage.
20. J	SENTENCE STRUCTURE	Choices F, G, and H all set up the proper sentence construction here: We begin with an incomplete thought (called a subordinate clause) paired with a complete thought (call an independent clause). The comma between these two clauses links them together. Now, look at choice J. The word *yet* belongs to a category called coordinating conjunctions (think of the acronym FANBOYS: for, and, nor, but, or, yet, so). Just as you wouldn't use the word *but* or *and* at the beginning of this sentence, *yet* doesn't belong here, either (coordinating conjunctions are used in the middle of a sentence to join two complete thoughts).
21. A	WORD CHOICE	The second half of this sentence serves to offer a contrast between the first half of the sentence or to offer a clarification, which choices A, C, and D do. Choice A does not fit because the word *meanwhile* is used to show two actions occurring simultaneously, which is not the intention of this sentence.
22. H	PUNCTUATION	Choice F creates a sentence fragment, and choice G has an incorrect word choice with *though*. Choice J is incorrect because we would need a comma before clauses that begin with the word *which*. Choice H is correct because we do not need a comma before clauses beginning with the word *that*.
23. C	WORDINESS & REDUNDANCY	Choices A, B, and D all contains pairs of words that are similar in meaning to one another and, therefore, unnecessarily wordy and redundant. Choice C, however, is the most simple and concise. Remember, the ACT likes writing that is to the point.
24. F	SENTENCE STRUCTURE	The conjunction *and* adds emphasis and further enhances the listing of items in the sentence. G, H, and J are incorrect because the words make it sound like furniture and appliances are types of clothing and dishes.
25. D	SENTENCE STRUCTURE	Choice A is wrong because the semicolon is used incorrectly; the second half of the sentence is not a complete thought. Choice B is incorrect because *realizes* does not agree with the plural noun *environmentalists*. Choice C is incorrect because the object pronoun *whom* does not agree with the subject *environmentalists*.
26. F	WORDINESS AND REDUNDANCY	Choices B, C, and D are too similar in meaning and therefore redundant when paired with *resources*. *Energy* (choice F), however, provides different and additional information.
27. B	ORGANIZATION	The main focus of this paragraph is about motivation for people to adopt a freegan lifestyle, which is introduced in broad terms in sentence 2. Anti-materialism (sentence 4), fulfilling work (sentence 5), and how they furnish their homes (sentence 1) are all supporting details of sentence 2.

28. H	ADDING & DELETING INFORMATION	The final paragraph focuses on less extreme measures people could take towards a more freegan-inspired lifestyle. The inclusion of the word *perhaps* implies this suggestive tone and possible recommendations the reader could try.
29. D	PRONOUN REFERENCE/WORD CHOICE	The expression *get dumped* is slang and should be avoided (choice A). Choice B contains a contraction (*it's* stands for *it is,* which doesn't make sense here). Choice C uses the wrong pronoun reference, incorrectly using the singular *it* to refer to the plural antecedent *day old bread and other item.*
30. G	ORGANIZATION	Sentence 2 introduces the topic of this paragraph (small steps to take towards freeganism) while also transitioning from the previous paragraph. Based off of the process of elimination, this alone helps us to eliminate choice F, H, and J. However, it's still a good idea to make sure the remaining order of sentences makes sense. Sentences 1 and 3 would be next, as they provide support details that illustrate the main idea presented in sentence 1. Finally, the paragraph should end with sentence 4, which ends with a memorable concluding statement that would wrap up the paragraph and the passage as a whole.

ANSWER	SKILL(S)	EXPLANATION
31. D	PUNCTUATION	Use the dash to offset the explanatory phrase. A semicolon (choice A) does not work because what follows it is not a complete thought. A colon (choice B) could possibly work here, EXCEPT that in choice B, the word after the colon is incorrectly capitalized.
32. H	WORD CHOICE/ SENTENCE STRUCTURE	The word *although* shows a contrast between the first and second halves of the sentence. Choices F, G, and J are incorrect because we are not showing a cause-and effect relationship (students do not take similar general education courses <u>because</u> they have different majors).
33. D	PUNCTUATION	Offset the word *however* with commas to separate it from the complete thought it interrupts. Notice that if we remove the word *however*, the sentence would still express a complete thought and would make sense. Choice C incorrectly uses the semicolon. Semicolons are used to join two complete thoughts, but the first half of the sentence before the semicolon in choice C is actually a fragment.
34. F	ADDING & REVISING INFORMATION	The main theme of the passage is that many college classes are interesting and enjoyable, a sentiment best expressed by choice F. Each of the other choices do not follow the direction of the paragraph as it changes from college being about subjects and studying to something different.
35. A	SENTENCE STRUCTURE	You may be used to inserting a comma after "in addition" when it appears at the beginning of a sentence as an introductory transition. However, that's NOT how "in addition" is being used in this sentence. Instead, it is part of a longer introductory phrase: "In addition to studying the traditional canon of Shakespeare, Dickens, and Homer…" The comma should go after this whole phrase, offsetting it from the complete thought that follows.
36. F	WORD CHOICE	This question deals with idioms, expressions that do not easily translate over into other languages. Choice G is incorrect because in English, we read *about* something, we don't read *of* something. In choice H, the preposition *for* sounds odd in the expression—you have an option *of* something, not an option *for* something. Choice J may sound all right, but F is the better option: *reading* is more consistent with the verb *studying* used earlier in the paragraph.
37. C	WORD CHOICE	The sentence can be read as either providing an additional example of an unusual college class (choice B) or showing differences between different types of course offerings (choices A and D). Choice C, *as*, distorts these meanings because we don't know if these different courses are being run simultaneously.
38. G	WORD CHOICE	The sentence is intended to show the different classifications of classes about *The Simpsons* at different universities. Choice G would not fit because it changes the meaning by pointing out a similarity.
39. B	SENTENCE STRUCTURE	This one may seem tricky. Grammatically speaking, sentences should not begin with the word *and*. However, here you need to consider the style, tone, and author's intention with this paragraph and the passage as a whole. The passage is not written in an overly formal style. Consider how the paragraph would sound without the word *and*—the last sentence would just be another example, and it wouldn't have any kind of transition to tie it in with the previous example. Here, the word *and* at the beginning of the sentence gives the example more weight and additional importance and emphasis that fits with the style of the passage as a whole.
40. G	WORD CHOICE	The word *instead* (choice G) presents an alternative to the idea expressed in the previous sentence. Choice F doesn't make sense because the sentence isn't really offering a clarification. The word *rather* (choice H) should be part of the expression *rather than* to show a comparison. Choice J doesn't have a transition, and the author's purpose isn't necessarily to make recommendations to the reader, but simply to provide information.

105

41. D	WORD CHOICE	Choice A sounds too "surfer dude." Choice B is a bit wordy and is missing the necessary commas to offset it from the rest of the sentence. Choice C is redundant (the word *serious* is already in the sentence). Choice D is correct because it contrasts what sounds like a joke with the real, actual class.
42. F	SENTENCE STRUCTURE	Choice J maintains parallel structure by listing three similar nouns. While choice G also has parallel structure, it is also redundant by adding the word "issues" to the end ("issues" also appears before the list). A great rule of thumb on the ACT English is "If it isn't broken, don't fix it" (NO CHANGE).
43. A	SENTENCE STRUCTURE	Choice A correctly uses the conjunction *and* with a comma that precedes it to join two complete thoughts.
44. J	SENTENCE STRUCTURE	Choices F, G, and H all contain a clause or phrase that elaborates on the effects of these classes. Choice J, though, alters that meaning by shifting the focus from the classes themselves to the students.
45. B	ORGANIZATION	The sentence provides examples of video games, which would best fit in paragraph 3, which mentions the use of video games in college classes.

106

ANSWER	SKILL(S)	EXPLANATION
46. H	WORDINESS & REDUNDANCY	Choice F should be eliminated because it is overly wordy. Choice G doesn't work because no one is requiring teenage boys to come up with prom proposals. Choice J also doesn't fit because prom proposals are really an obstacle or something that stands in the way of a boy getting a date. Choice H, *task*, is the best choice because it conveys a job or an action to be completed.
47. D	SENTENCE STRUCTURE	Begin the sentence with the subject, "Prom proposals," followed by the verb *have increased*. ACT typically prefers a straight-forward sentence structure that clearly states the subject first, followed by the verb, then any additional objects, modifiers, etc.
48. G	WORD CHOICE	*Possible* (choice F), *prospective* (choice H), and *probable* (choice J) are similar in meaning to the original wording in the passage, *potential*. *Perpetual* (choice G), though, is different in meaning; *perpetual* means "ongoing."
49. D	SENTENCE STRUCTURE	The word *while* in choice D doesn't fit; *while* shows either time sequence or a contrast, neither of which work here.
50. G	WORDINESS & REDUNDANCY	The simplest and most concise option is choice G. The main idea of the paragraph suggests proposals becoming more public, not including everyone (choice H).
51. D	WORDINESS & REDUNDANCY	The simplest and most concise option is choice D.
52. G	ADDING INFORMATION	Choice G provides the most appropriate wrap-up for the various examples of outrageous prom proposals outlined in the previous sentence.
53. C	SUBJECT & OBJECT PRONOUNS	Ignore *his friends* for a moment. Now, the subject pronoun *he* is obviously the best choice. This technique of ignoring the other person or group can often lead us to the correct subject pronoun.
54. G	SENTENCE STRUCTURE	F should be eliminated because it incorrectly uses a comma; you do not need a comma before a verb phrase. H is incorrect because it does not includes the necessary comma before the word *which*. Choice J should be eliminated because it sounds like the students stood in the entrance and greeted students as they entered the school.
55. D	SENTENCE STRUCTURE	Choice D sets the sentence up into two components: the first half of the sentence shows the girl's reaction, contrasted by the second half of the sentence, which contains the school's reaction. The word *while* emphasizes this contrast.
56. H	SENTENCE STRUCTURE	The main clause of the sentence is "The student was suspended." The phrase "along with his friends who helped him" contains extra information that interrupts this complete thought; therefore, the phrase should be offset with commas. Also, be sure to think about subject verb agreement in situations like this.
57. C	SENTENCE STRUCTURE	Choice A should be eliminated because it contains a run-on sentence. Choice B attempts to correct the run-on sentence, but it is unclear to whom the pronoun *they* refers. The underlined portion should not be omitted (choice D) because specifying that the young man had good intentions explains why people thought the punishment was too severe.
58. H	WORD CHOICE	The expression *for urging* (choice H) does not exist in English; we either *urge* someone to do something, or something is set up in order *to urge* someone to do something.
59. C	WORD CHOICE	The sentence intends to show that the punishment was lifted after a period of time. Choices A, B, and D do not accomplish this, but choice C does.
60. F	ADDING INFORMATION	Choice F provides closure for the anecdote about the student with the controversial proposal and reinforces the theme of the passage that prom proposals are intended to be memorable.

ANSWER KEY AND EXPLANATIONS

ANSWER	SKILL(S)	EXPLANATION
61. C	WORDINESS & REDUNDANCY	Choice C is the most straightforward and concise. When given a valid option that avoids wordiness, it's your best bet. Just be sure that it's a correct option.
62. J	PUNCTUATION	Put a comma after *books* to offset the phrase "along with the popular *Twilight* film series and books."
63. A	WORD CHOICE	Any high school age reader would know that vampires are real, so this statement isn't surprising (choice B) but rather obvious (choice A). It really isn't interesting (choice C) or important (choice D) that these creatures are fictional.
64. H	WORD CHOICE	*Twi-hards* (choice F) is a slang term for fans of *Twilight,* but the passage doesn't focus on only that one vampire story. Choice G is a bit unclear, and Choice J doesn't work because the sentence would be left without a subject.
65. B	PUNCTUATION	The main clause of the sentence, "Many fans of the genre may be surprised to learn that the most well-known vampire of all has his roots in true history" is interrupted by the phrase "the one and only Dracula." Offset this interruption with commas.
66. F	SENTENCE STRUCTURE	The appositive "Bram Stoker" is essential; without it, it would be unclear whom "author" refers to. Therefore do not offset it with a comma—this makes choice F the exception and hence our answer.
67. C	ADDING & DELETING INFORMATION	At the end of the paragraph, the author references modern-day Romania. It is helpful, then, to explain that Transylvania and Romania refer to the same place.
68. J	PUNCTUATION	The conjunction *and* links two complete thoughts. When a conjunction links two complete thoughts, put a comma before the conjunction. Choice H is incorrect because we should not use a semicolon and conjunctions like *and* together. A semicolon alone is fine and when used with a conjunctive adverb like *however* or *therefore*.
69. C	VERB TENSE	The present participle *committing* (choice C) is missing a helping verb, making it incorrect. Reading a sentence through can sometimes reveal an answer.
70. H	WORDINESS & REDUNDANCY	*Contemporary* and *current* are synonyms and, therefore, the expression is redundant. Choice H expresses the idea in more concise terms.
71. D	PUNCTUATION	Colons are for introducing lists and are used after statements that are complete sentences. There is no use for a colon here. No punctuation is required (choice D) for this question.
72. H	WORDINESS & REDUNDANCY	*Malicious, agonizing,* and *brutal* are similar in intensity, whereas *irate* downplays the viciousness of Vlad's means of torture. *Irate* means irritated or annoyed, which underscores the extent of Vlad's rage and cruelty.
73. A	PUNCTUATION	There is no need to separate the prepositional phrase "in his ruthless quest from power" from the rest of the sentence, so no punctuation is needed.
74. G	PUNCTUATION	The original version creates a sentence fragment; to fix it, attach the fragment to the rest of the sentence with a comma.
75. C	STYLE & RHETORIC	Although the first paragraph mentions the current popularity of vampires in popular culture, that is not the focus of the passage.

ANSWER	SKILL(S)	EXPLANATION
1. D	DRAWING CONCLUSIONS	A smirk often suggests self-satisfaction or smugness. At this point in Jerry's story, he is probably bragging to his audience that after their little kiss, the girl wants to leave with him. Options A and C are inconsistent with a smirk, and there is no indication in the passage that the story is a lie or hoax (B).
2. F	MAIN IDEA	The focus of the passage is really about Jerry and his story. The main point is to see Jerry's reactions and false frustrations when his friends are asking for his story. It seems like Jerry is enjoying the attention and is hesitant only to keep his friends begging. Although the setting is established (G), it isn't the main point of the first 3 paragraphs. This is about getting to know who Jerry is, not learning about the bar he frequents.
3. A	DRAWING CONCLUSIONS	Jerry respects the girl's opinions on what street to take home (lines 51-53), pulls over for the girl (line 63), and offers to escort the girl walk to wherever she's going (lines 66-68). It may be considered forward to some readers for him to go for a kiss when dancing (C), but he doesn't necessarily persuade her from doing something she doesn't want to do.
4. J	DRAWING CONCLUSIONS	After the intensity of Jerry's tale, the customers return to their typical actions. The author writes that they take a gasp of air to emphasize their deep attention. Option G suggests a break, but at this point, the story is complete.
5. C	WORD MEANING	The term "shoot warnings" has a contrasting meaning with the laughter that precedes it. If some are laughing, others are not amused by the interruption. These people are likely giving mean looks to signal not to interrupt Jerry again. There is nothing spoken (A and D), and who in their right mind would fire a handgun over an interruption (B)?
6. H	DRAWING CONCLUSIONS / WORD MEANING	Especially demonstrated in the final few paragraphs, they all seem to respect one another as friends and acquaintances would. Jerry and his audience don't exhibit an avoiding attitude (F), and are only joking when they tease each other or showing frustration and not showing open hostility (G). Though the audience does show a bit of relief at the end of the story, the members do not show this kind of attitude toward Jerry.
7. B	AUTHOR'S PURPOSE	The casual setting of a local bar or pub and a group of patrons familiar with each other is highlighted though the author's inclusion of casual, vernacular words and conversation. Casual phrasing and speech can also suggest a level of intelligence (C) in certain situations, but keep in mind that he is not lawyer in the courtroom or president giving a speech using these phrases. He's simply a guy at a bar telling his friends a favorite story.
8. F	SUPPORTING DETAILS	Though the ghost has a white dress, nowhere in the passage does Jerry suggest it was glowing—a white glow or fog is commonly associated with ghosts. Icy lips are demonstrated in line 35, cold hands exist in line 44, and her escape to the cemetery is shown in lines 75-79.
9. C	SUPPORTING DETAILS	Options A, B, and D all suggest that Jerry's audience is eager to hear that story and even start begging him. They immediately focus on the story because they are looking forward to hearing every word. Option C has nothing to do with the customers' desire to hear the tale.
10. F	DRAWING CONCLUSIONS	Multiple times during his story, Jerry is said to be wiping or rubbing his glass (lines 54 and 80). Unconscious fidgeting is often thought to accompany anxiety. Jerry does not have a sudden desire to leave; in fact, he even suggested he wished to go before he started his story (G). There is no specific connection between his casual speech and his grin and twinkle in his eye (H and J) and any anxiety he may be feeling.

ANSWER KEY AND EXPLANATIONS

ANSWER	SKILL(S)	EXPLANATION
11. D	AUTHOR'S PURPOSE	Repeatedly the author explains that this particular technology has changed the way we live. A few examples include sleep deprivation, safety concerns, and ease of communication with others.
12. G	MAIN IDEA	Ask yourself, "What is the point of including this paragraph?" It really serves the purpose of easing up on the doom and gloom from the previous paragraphs (sleep loss and driving safety) and incorporates how texting can be a form of competition and entertainment. Option F is incorrect because not everyone who can text particularly well will find fame and fortune. Option H may appear to be a strong option; however, is the main purpose of the paragraph truly about how people are brought together like the Olympics? It is more about the fun of texting than bringing people together. Option J is incorrect because it includes the absolute *always*. Technology doesn't ALWAYS bring people together for events.
13. D	AUTHOR'S PURPOSE / WORD MEANING	We not only have to know what the words mean, but also determine what the author thinks about sign language. *Uncomplicated* means, "not involving complication." *Cryptic* means, "having a secret or mysterious meaning." *Maddening* means, "tending to make angry." *Antiquated* means, "Old-fashioned or obsolete." Based on the first paragraph and particularly lines 10-12 state that signing should "move aside" for texting, which suggests that texting is a better way to communicate. That should point to *antiquated*, something that is obsolete and not useful anymore.
14. F	SUPPORTING DETAILS	Be careful of this NOT question. Option G is clear in paragraph 5, option H apparent in paragraph 3, and option J exists in paragraph 2. Nowhere does the passage suggest new technology reduces the amount of time spent talking to people face-to-face, even if you think that may be true.
15. A	AUTHOR'S PURPOSE	The author uses the term in order to emphasize the trouble a teen may get into for going over the limits of the monthly phone contract. No one's life was literally in danger if he or she had a high bill (D). The term is not a warning (B) or a threat to listen to parents (C).
16. H	SUPPORTING DETAILS	Paragraph 2 explains that Neil Papworth of Sema Group used the first person-to-person texting technology. Richard Jarvis (F) only received this first message. Vodafone (G) was the network he used, but this network was not responsible for developing text messaging, as the question asks. Kate Moore (J) is a teen who showed her abilities with the technology.
17. C	DRAWING CONCLUSIONS	The statement in question deals only with the fact that lives are negatively affected by technology. It is too extreme to say teens are so concerned about every single text message that they become frightened to miss one and don't worry about sleep (B).
18. J	AUTHOR'S PURPOSE	By breaking down the daily rate of texting for Kate Moore, a teen who texts a great deal more than an average teenager, the author is demonstrating how texts per day add up to a very large number. Sure, practice makes perfect, but certainly Moore did more than text her friends to train for a competition (G). We cannot assume that a large number of daily texts is the only reason she is a champion texter.
19. A	WORD MEANING	*Assayed* means, "an analysis or examination." We can use the general idea of the sentence to develop context clues. Studies were looking at, or examined, the impact of frequent texting on teens.
20.	AUTHOR'S PURPOSE	In the last paragraph, the author moves from a passage about SMS technology and communication to a general idea about technology bringing people together. This is especially apparent in lines 94-97. Even though texting can be a problem for some (F), this a very specific circumstance—the passage isn't an examination of how technology can ruin the world. Option G uses the absolute *all*, and there is little evidence that all technology should only be given to responsible citizens.

ANSWER KEY AND EXPLANATIONS

ANSWER	SKILL(S)	EXPLANATION
21. A	DRAWING CONCLUSIONS	Line 49 describes PewDiePie's humor as "juvenile" and "obnoxious." The word *annoying* would best describe the author's feelings toward this YouTube sensation.
22. J	SUPPORTING DETAILS	Information in paragraph 1 explains that 80% of U.S. teens and 70% of U.S. millennials use YouTube. There is no information about how many gamers or musicians view videos on the site.
23. B	SUPPORTING DETAILS / SEQUENCE	Line 36 states that "Gangnam Style" (A) was uploaded in July 2012. "Blank Space" was posted 8 months after "Dark Horse," (D) which was posted in February 2014. "Evolution of Dance" is nearly a decade old, as lines 66-67 explain.
24. F	AUTHOR'S PURPOSE	Expository writing (F) is writing to inform or explain the subject, which is what the author is attempting to do. Persuasive writing (G) attempts to influence the reader; he is not trying to make the reader believe his opinion. Narrative writing (H) is a form of writing that tells a story. Descriptive writing (J) incorporates a great number of details in efforts to paint a picture and incorporate the reader's senses.
25. B	DRAWING CONCLUSIONS	Though the likes and dislikes may show people don't like the song, these do not tell the whole story. With 1.2 billion views compared to 5 million dislikes, there are clearly many more fans who come to view the video than haters. In actuality, those 5 million visitors who just came to spread hate about Bieber are actually helping him retain popularity and his YouTube ranking.
26. H	MAIN IDEA	The main idea is best expressed in the last sentence of the paragraph (lines 73-75) and somewhat in the first sentence (lines 59-60) when contrasting the previous paragraphs of those who sought fame.
27. C	WORD MEANING	Sometimes placing the options in the place of the target word can lead a reader to the correct answer. In this case, Bieber didn't corrupt people to like his video (A), nor did he mislead or trick them into visiting his song (D). Some may strongly dislike Bieber, but loath (B) does not make sense in context. The best choice here happens to be the one that is straightforward and clear.
28. G	AUTHOR'S PURPOSE	By comparing "Gangnam Style" to other popular songs, the author is able to demonstrate just how successful Psy's song has been over time. Psy's average is still better than the all-time ratings of some very successful songs. Nowhere does the article suggest that these are favorite artists of the author (F) and certainly ACT practice material is not intended to be publicity for any artist. We cannot be sure these other songs are part of the top ten list (H), and level of talent is not suggested either.
29. B	DRAWING CONCLUSIONS	Lines 53-54 state that Sky Does Minecraft has a similar commentary style and gameplay to VanossGaming and PewDiePie. These channels were described as humorous and include playing with friends. Line 49, though, states that the high pitched screaming is unique to PewDiePie, which makes option B the only possible choice.
30. H	SUPPORTING DETAILS	Lines 23-24 state that "Blank Space" has an eight month deficit, or difference, from "Dark Horse," which was posted in February 2014. Eight months after February is November.

	ANSWER	SKILL(S)	EXPLANATION
ANSWER KEY AND EXPLANATIONS	**31. C**	**WORD MEANING/ AUTHOR'S PURPOSE**	Tone is an author's attitude when writing. Think about writing tone as similar to tone of voice when feeling emotions, such as anger, sadness, or happiness. *Apathetic* means lack of concern (A), *idealistic* means hoping for perfection (B), *forthright* means direct and without hesitation (C), and *hesitant* means slow to act (D). The author seems to focus on changing things and getting things done. The best word to describe this type of tone is *forthright* because he is giving the facts and demanding change. He's not living in a dream world of perfection (A) or waiting to see what will happen (D).
	32. G	**AUTHOR'S PURPOSE**	Though there is plenty of information with facts and percentages, the purpose is not simply to give us information. With phrasing like, "We must start looking," (line 82) and "for it is imperative to start," (line 98), the author is attempting to persuade the reader into thinking as he does and inspire readers to action.
	33. B	**SUPPORTING DETAILS**	Option A is shown in lines 37-39, option C is shown in line 40, and option D is shown in lines 36-37. The author hints at possible starvation from lack of resources (lines 43-45), but that doesn't mean extinction. Option B is the best choice for this EXCEPT question.
	34. G	**AUTHOR'S PURPOSE**	Reread lines 83-95, the water usage example. The author likely wishes to make readers aware of their wasteful daily habits and think about changing them. Option G suggests changing something beyond what the author would consider wasteful and is the best choice for this NOT question.
	35. A	**WORD MEANING**	The question is asking the reader to determine the meaning of the phrase presented. Be careful, though, because the passage uses the word *not* in front of the phrase, where in the question, it is simply the phrase, "out of our hands." The paragraph goes on to provide smaller ideas to change individual people's habits, so the phrase most likely means "an area an individual cannot control" (A).
	36. J	**AUTHOR'S PURPOSE**	The passage is persuasive, provides many different details, and suggests alternatives to common wasteful habits. A passage like this doesn't suggest specific ways to change industry (F), cannot provide enough non-biased information for a research report (G), or give enough detail about alternatives to common pollutants. The best choice is option J because the passage provides some general information and provides some solutions—it's not in depth or specific enough for the other choices.
	37. B	**SUPPORTING DETAILS**	Use the information in lines 59-62 to solve this question. If 12 foot wall of waste paper = 50 million tons of consumed paper, and If 50 million tons of consumed paper = 850 million trees, then 850 million trees must equal 12 foot wall of waste paper stretched across the nation.
	38. H	**DRAWING CONCLUSIONS**	Lines 15-16 suggest the correct answer, that the author feels humans are plaguing the Earth and can potentially kill it. There is no statement against the Industrial Revolution (F), no suggestion of a coming war for land and food (G), and no suggested alternative planet in which humans can live (J).
	39. A	**AUTHOR'S PURPOSE**	Don't be intimidated by the question and lengthy answer choices. Option B discusses a connection to film, but doesn't actually explain why the author would use this type of writing construction. Option C stops at Americans and doesn't address the individual. Option D sounds possible, but uses the absolute "every single individual" as a cause and solution to the problems.
	40. J	**DRAWING CONCLUSIONS**	Since the question is focused on breathing, eliminate options G and H as possibilities. Option F suggests some kind place we can go to, but clearly the passage is referring to the fact that without plants and their ability to release oxygen through photosynthesis.

112

ANSWER	SKILL(S)	EXPLANATION
1. B	PUNCTUATION	Multiple fans would have more than one favorite player, so *players* should be plural. The word *numbers*, then, would be plural too. Now, let's go back to *players*. Not only is the noun plural, it is also possessive because the passage is discussing THEIR numbers. An ending of *–s'* indicates plural-possessive. There is no need for an apostrophe on *numbers* because the numbers do not own anything—it's simply a plural noun.
2. H	PRONOUN REFERENCE	The antecedent is *fans*, which is plural, and in this sentence, also possessive, making *their* the best fit.
3. D	SENTENCE STRUCTURE	The head coach IS a multi-millionaire; we're not talking about two separate people here. Therefore, take out the conjunction *and*. While Choices B and C also express this idea, they are not punctuated correctly and are overly wordy.
4. J	WORD CHOICE	In order to use *for the privilege of*, the following word would have to be *broadcasting*, but the passage uses *broadcast*, which means choice J does not fit.
5. C	WORD CHOICE	The word *yet* expresses a contrast, similar to *however* (choice A), *conversely* (choice B), and *on the other hand* (choice D). Choice C changes the meaning of the sentence.
6. J	WORD CHOICE	Choices F, G, and H show a cause and effect relationship, which emphasizes the reason that student athletes are exempt from compensation as stated in the second half of the sentence. Choice J does not emphasize this cause and effect relationship.
7. B	WORD CHOICE	The word *dumb* is too casual to use in this argumentative yet academic article. Choice C, *disrespectful*, suggests that the schools and NCAA do not respect the players, but the paragraph is really about athletes getting their fair share. Choice D, *tolerable*, is opposite in meaning from what the paragraph is trying to suggest.
8. G	PRONOUN REFERENCE	The pronoun *everyone* is a bit ambiguous in this case. Money is generated for the university by the college athletes; choice G makes this clearer.
9. B	WORD CHOICE	The phrase is referring back to *the life* of an athlete, which is singular, making *that* a better fit than *those*.
10. H	SENTENCE STRUCTURE	Choice H maintains parallel structure by listing three similarly-structured verbs: *working*, *practicing*, and *studying*.
11. B	WORD CHOICE	The paragraph is shifting from showing the lack of compensation college athletes receive in contrast to the hefty salaries their coaches earn. *In contrast* most directly highlights this contrast and maintains the more formal style of the passage.
12. J	SENTENCE STRUCTURE	The sentence is a run on sentence without a comma before the conjunction *and*. There is no reason to use a colon here (choice G), and choice H is not a properly formed fix for a run on (would need a semicolon before *therefore* for this to be correct). The only correct option is forming two sentences.
13. D	WORD CHOICE	The simplest and most parallel wording would be *not a paycheck*. This serves as a direct comparison to the preceding direct object, *a degree*.
14. J	AGREEMENT	The word *funds* should agree with the verb *is used*. When the subject and verb get separated with other information, it is easy to forget about agreement with the true subject. Take out the extra information and test again—funds *are* used.
15. C	ADDING INFORMATION	The passage looks at both sides of the issue, and choice C is the least biased.

	ANSWER	SKILL(S)	EXPLANATION
ANSWER KEY AND EXPLANATIONS	16. G	WORD CHOICE	*Common* and *ordinary* are redundant, so choice F should be eliminated. Choices H and J are overly wordy and too casual, so G is the best fit.
	17. A	WORD CHOICE	The passage focuses on how senior pranks are becoming more prevalent, which the word *increasingly* implies.
	18. H	WORD CHOICE	Beginning the sentence with *but* would create a sentence fragment.
	19. C	SENTENCE STRUCTURE	The second half of the sentence in the original sentence is a sentence fragment. This can be corrected by joining the fragment to the complete thought that precedes it with a comma.
	20. F	WORD CHOICE	*Appropriately* emphasizes the connection between the title and the content of the show.
	21. D	SENTENCE STRUCTURE	The original sentence is incorrect because it forgets to include a comma before the conjunction *and*, which connects two complete thoughts. Removing the pronoun *it* (choice D) fixes this problem.
	22. J	SENTENCE STRUCTURE	Unless it is a proper noun, do not capitalize the word after a semicolon. Also, we do not need a comma after *often* because there is already a comma after the complete phrase, *often times*.
	23. B	PRONOUN REFERENCE	The antecedent is the plural noun *pranks*; choice B uses the correct pronoun *they* and avoids the unnecessary addition of *will* from choice C.
	24. H	WORD CHOICE	Here, the author is discussing the focus or the topic of the prank, which would best be expressed with the word *about* (choice H). The joke is not *on* the animals (choice F), *for the* animals (choice G), or *concerning* the animals (choice J).
	25. B	PUNCTUATION	Choice B is wrong because there is no separation between the example and the main thought of the sentence.
	26. J	WORD CHOICE	The word *unwittingly* implies gullibility.
	27. B	WORD CHOICE	We are looking for a contrast to the word *funny*, which would be *serious*. This is further reinforced by the example that follows.
	28. G	WORD CHOICE	This paragraph provides another example of a prank turned serious. The word *conversely* would mark a shift that would be of a different theme, whereas the author intends to illustrate a similarity.
	29. D	ADDING & REVISING INFORMATION	The author does not really take a position on whether or not pranks should be done; the revision would not fit because it contains a bias not found in the rest of the passage.
	30. H	STYLE & RHETORIC	The author doesn't discuss the "best" pranks, but rather explores a current phenomenon and the possible pros and cons of such pranks.

114

ANSWER	SKILL(S)	EXPLANATION
31. A	ADJECTIVES & ADVERBS	The adverb *intentionally* (choice A) is needed to describe HOW the style gave the impression. The verb *to giving* in choice C doesn't make sense, though intentional style does.
32. H	PUNCTUATION	*Movies* should contain an apostrophe before the *-s* because it is singular and possessive (the characters "belong to" the movie, in a sense). *Characters*, however, is plural but NOT possessive, so it does not need an apostrophe.
33. B	MISPLACED MODIFIER	Typically, movies are filmed by a director. In this example, though, the move is different because it appears that the characters are doing the filming. This contrast is best highlighted by putting the phrase "not a director" directly after "the movie's principal characters." When given the chance, we should place relating information as close as possible to the other.
34. J	WORDINESS	Choice F is too wordy. Choice G doesn't make sense (someone isn't "unknown" if he or she is "famous"). Choice H is too vague—are these actors known or not? Choice J is the most concise and direct.
35. A	SENTENCE STRUCTURE	Offset the introductory phrase from the complete thought that follows with a comma.
36. H	WORD CHOICE	The word *predecessor* means something that comes before another work.
37. C	PRONOUN REFERENCE	The antecedent is the singular film title *The Blair Witch Project*. The word *its* fits this singular, possessive, gender-neutral antecedent. Be sure to select the possessive form of *its*, without an apostrophe (versus i*t's*, which is a contraction for "it is").
38. G	SUBJECT-VERB AGREEMENT	Even though *1990s* may sound plural, it is actually referring to a singular decade, so select the verb *was* to agree with the singular subject.
39. A	PUNCTUATION	There is no need for punctuation between the word *like* and the examples that follow.
40. H	ORGANIZATION	Paragraph 4 first brings us to the time frame of the 1990s, which is subsequently explored in more detail in paragraph 3.
41. B	ADDING & REVISING INFORMATION	Choice B reinforces the main idea of the paragraph about what made *The Blair Witch Project* so successful in the horror genre.
42. J	SENTENCE STRUCTURE	Put a comma before the conjunction *but* when it connects two complete thoughts.
43. B	WORD CHOICE	The paragraph focuses on the emerging horror movie genre in the aftermath of *Blair Witch* and studios' attempts to bring more films to interested audiences. Japanese films were remade to be adapted for American audiences.
44. H	WORD CHOICE	The word *stagnant* best conveys something old, stale, and unchanging.
45. C	PRONOUN REFERENCE	The antecedent is the plural noun *ideas*; the pronoun *they* is the best fit to reference that antecedent.

ANSWER KEY AND EXPLANATIONS

ANSWER KEY AND EXPLANATIONS

ANSWER	SKILL(S)	EXPLANATION
46. J	WORDINESS & REDUNDANCY	We don't really need to know when the term "flash mob" came into existence, so for the sake of clarity and conciseness, go ahead and omit it.
47. A	MISPLACED MODIFIER	The prepositional phrase "of people in a public space" serves to describe the *gathering*, so eliminate choice B, which would interrupt the phrase from what it describes. The underlined portion is not intended to modify the word *describe,* so eliminate choice C. However, we do not want to omit the underlined portion entirely (choice D) because it contains essential information about what makes flash mobs so spontaneous and surprising. Therefore, A is the best option.
48. H	ADDING & DELETING INFORMATION	Flash mobs may seem spontaneous and spur-of-the-moment, but the fact that they actually well-planned and rehearsed is surprising. This word helps to fully explain their appeal.
49. C	PRONOUN REFERENCE	The pronoun is intended to refer to the subject *mobbers*. However, *they* is too ambiguous; the word *participants* makes it more clear whom exactly is being referred to.
50. G	WORD CHOICE	The word *but* highlights the contrast between the common and more unexpected appearances of pillow fights.
51. B	VERB TENSE	Due to the other present tense verbs in this paragraph (*are, gather*), maintain consistent verb tense by selecting the present tense verb *are joining*.
52. J	MISPLACED MODIFIER	The modifier should be placed after "pillow fight" in order to describe the purpose behind the pillow fight.
53. A	WORD CHOICE	The present tense verb phrase *has taken on* indicates we are talking about a present-day movement. The word *as* (Choice A) would correctly indicate two events occurring simultaneously.
54. G	VERB TENSE	Choice G maintains consistent verb tense; they *kayaked* across the river at the same time they *stormed* the city.
55. D	REVISING INFORMATION	*Boring* takes on a different meaning than *the norm, normal, expected*, and *ordinary*.
56. J	WORDINESS & REDUNDANCY	*Poke fun at* and *mock* mean the same thing; only one word needs to be used.
57. B	WORD CHOICE	*However* shows a shift between the original intent of flash mobs and the different form they take today.
58. J	VERB TENSE	Similar to the previously used verb *had, used* fulfills the need to use the past tense throughout the paragraph.
59. C	PUNCTUATION	The passage is referring to a singular company, T Mobile. It is possessive, though, because the commercials belong to the company. Therefore, choose the singular possessive noun.

60. G	**ORGANIZATION**	First, figure out which paragraph would make the best introduction. It would be paragraph 2 (G and H) because all of the other paragraphs begin with a reference to an idea that was mentioned in another paragraph. Now, decide which paragraph should be second—either Paragraph 1 (G) or Paragraph 4 (H). Paragraph 2 provides an example of a flash mob; notice that paragraph 1 begins with, "This is just one example of the modern day phenomenon known as a flash mob." This makes Paragraph 1 the next logical choice, making choice G our answer.

ANSWER	SKILL(S)	EXPLANATION
61. B	PUNCTUATION	When two adjectives (like *straight-A* and *intelligent*) are interchangeable, put a comma between them. However, when you have fewer than three adjectives, you do not need a comma after the last adjective.
62. G	PUNCTUATION	The expression "needless to say" is an interruption to the main clause of the sentence; offset it with commas.
63. D	SENTENCE STRUCTURE	Begin the sentence with the subject, *Lil Wayne* (choices B, C, and D). The verb *released* should come next (choices B and D), followed by the direct object "his first double platinum solo album" (choice D).
64. J	WORDINESS & REDUNDANCY	Earlier, the paragraph gives us the date *1997*. Since the passage then tells us his album was released *two years later*, we do not need to be explicitly told the year 1999; the date can be omitted.
65. B	VERB TENSE	The simple past tense verb *released* is consistent with the other usage of *released* earlier in the paragraph.
66. H	WORD CHOICE	Choice F should be eliminated because it incorrectly uses the plural form of *freshmen* instead of the singular *freshman*. Choice G is incorrect because it uses the word *then* (which is used to show time order) instead of *than* (which shows comparison). The underlined portion should not be omitted because we need some sort of information to compare the sophomore effort to.
67. A	WORD CHOICE	The sentence intends to show what happened *when* Lil Wayne was featured on the Destiny's Child track (choice A). Choices B and C change the intended meaning and are also punctuated incorrectly. In choice D, the word *thus* does not work because the sentence doesn't show a cause and effect relationship.
68. J	ADJECTIVES AND ADVERBS	The adverb *instantly* modifies the verb *earned*. Choice G shows an absolute; if something is instant, it can't be MORE instant than it already is. Choice H is redundant with the word *almost*.
69. C	WORD CHOICE	The word *which* (choice C) is the best option to begin a clause that describes Wayne's talent and that serves as an interruption to the main clause of the sentence. *That* (choice B) should not have a comma before it.
70. G	ADDING & REVISING INFORMATION	The paragraph looks at the progression of Wayne's career and the development of his musical style. Choices F and J are too casual, opinionated, and don't fit the informative nature of the passage.
71. D	PUNCTUATION	There is no need for punctuation to separate any of the words in this phrase.
72. G	PUNCTUATION	*Album* is singular and possessive. Regular singular possessive nouns need a *'s* ending.
73. D	SENTENCE STRUCTURE	Attach the phrase at the end of the sentence to the complete thought that precedes it by using a comma when they act as "afterthoughts" to the main thought of the sentence. Choices A, B, and C leave a fragment starting with the word *spawning*.
74. G	ADDING AND REVISING INFORMATION	Choice G references the performances mentioned in the previous sentence and emphasizes his multi-genre appeal. Choices F and H are not proven facts, and choice J, once again, shows an opinion.
75. D	PUNCTUATION	A comma is needed to offset the dependent clause "when *Tha Carter IV* was released in 2011" from the complete thought that follows.

ANSWER	SKILL(S)	EXPLANATION
1. B	DRAWING CONCLUSIONS	It is revealed later when Stacy has her chance to explain that she was not interested in fighting, either; however, the crowd and mob mentality kicked in. Option B is the only option that supports Stacy's viewpoint; the others choices seem to be natural reactions if forced into a fight.
2. J	AUTHOR'S PURPOSE / DRAWING CONCLUSIONS	By including pictures of the dean's family, describing it as "warm and cozy," and contrasting it with a jail cell, the author intends to make the dean seem somewhat kind and friendly even before the reader has a chance to meet him. Option H suggests imagery, which is "vivid descriptions," but the description of the room is not exactly vivid. The purpose of describing the room is not to liven up a plain, boring passage, either.
3. A	DRAWING CONCLUSIONS	The term *ostracized* means "to exclude from friendships or society." Based upon her description in lines 97-104, the students at the school think Stacy is at fault. There is no indication that choices B and C will happen, and choice D seems unlikely. Choice A seems like the most likely effect of the conflict.
4. G	DRAWING CONCLUSIONS/ WORD MEANING	When practicing, it may be wise to keep a dictionary handy—it's better to learn unfamiliar words in preparation for the real test than get an "accurate" practice score. In these types of situations where two words are presented per choice, do your best to figure out one of the two. Option F—*Stalwart*: strong. *Unwavering*: unchanging. Option G—*Depressed*: low in spirits. *Dejected*: feeling unhappy Option H—*Egotistical*: overly confident, arrogant. *Self-centered*: concerned only with yourself. Option J—*Perplexed*: uncertain. *Baffled*: puzzled
5. A	AUTHOR'S PURPOSE	The lesson or moral of the story has to be about the concerns of posting information online as well as teen peer pressure. Readers may think if the secret weren't revealed, the whole fight wouldn't have happened—this may be true, but this is not the real message of the passage. If the girls actually had a chance to speak to each other and the other students didn't get involved, comment, etc., their friendship would have likely survived.
6. G	AUTHOR'S PURPOSE	Author's purpose questions can include author's technique, too. Familiarize yourself with the different types of narration while you continue to prepare. Option F suggests an omniscient protagonist, which means "an all-knowing main character." Lauren clearly doesn't know Stacy's thoughts. Think of an "objective observer" (H) as watching a movie—you can only see the actions of all characters without personal thoughts. We do get a glimpse of Lauren's thoughts within the dialogue. The narrator does not seem to try to hide much (J), so we wouldn't call her concealing. She is, however, biased since we see her viewpoint even though we find out she is wrong.
7. C	DRAWING CONCLUSIONS / WORD MEANING	The most likely choices are B and C since we see the dean does believe Lauren is the bully here (A) and there is no explanation of interrogation techniques in the passage (D). Though option B suggests events as they happen in sequence, the term "stared into my soul," (C) likely means his attempt to find something deeper about her.
8. G	DRAWING CONCLUSIONS / WORD MEANING	It is clear the mob of students made this fight physical. It wasn't friendly encouragement (F), but rather psychological and physical pressure (G) that made the girls meet up and then push each other.
9. D	DRAWING CONCLUSIONS	Based upon the narrator's version of the story, she was probably upset with her friend and found she could get even with her by revealing something about Stacy, but it doesn't seem that she wanted to end the friendship or bully her on Twitter.
10. J	DRAWING CONCLUSIONS	After Stacy tells her story, the narrator finally realizes that she was the problem all along. She ruined their friendship, was unintentionally a bully, and made her friend go through a horrible experience. She did not, however, have anything to do with starting a fight or involving the other students.

	ANSWER	SKILL(S)	EXPLANATION
ANSWER KEY AND EXPLANATIONS	11. D	SUPPORTING DETAILS	When questions like this get complicated, you can try making small organizers or drawings to help you keep track. Option D is the only possible choice because lines 29-30 state the AVERAGE over 6 samples must be less than 60, and D states a total number. 60 parts x 6 samples = 360 total parts, and 300 parts in total is less than 360, which makes this an acceptable number of insect parts.
	12. F	SUPPORTING DETAILS	Lines 65-67 clearly state Ohio University studied our accidental eating trends.
	13. B	WORD MEANING	*Perceptive* (B) means, "observant and aware," which is suggested by the antonyms "surprise and disgust" in line 11. *Sarcasm* (A) means, "a cutting remark usually meaning the opposite of what is said." *Crafty* (C) means, "skillful and clever," and *visionary* (D) means, "characterized by fancy or unworkable ideas or schemes."
	14. F	DRAWING CONCLUSIONS	Look to lines 50-54 to get an idea of the peanut butter allowable content (30+ is excessive) and combine that information with the FDA's statement in line 60 that food contains only about 10% of the excessive levels. 10% of 30 is 3 (math tip: to take 10% of something, drop the last digit), so the best choice is 2-3 (F).
	15. A	DRAWING CONCLUSIONS	The second-to-last paragraph (lines 70-90) gets into detail about reduction of levels, including pesticides and home farming options. Lines 75-77 suggest that there is no way to tell what insects you eat by growing food at home or local farm stands (B and D), and accepting a greater level of defects (C) is opposite of what the question is asking. Lines 81-83 and lines 86-89 support the correct answer, A.
	16. H	WORD MEANING	*Aesthetic* means, "the study or concern with beauty," so essentially, deals with something considered pleasing to the senses. Each of the other options are placed in contrast to the term in both of the sections where the word appears, probably to throw off the reader.
	17. B	SUPPORTING DETAILS	Nixon states that we should accept more insect parts in our food in efforts to reduce the harmful pesticides entering our body. He would NOT agree with increasing pesticides.
	18. G	MAIN IDEA	These are the real examples of insect and rodent parts in the foods we eat (chocolate, popcorn, and peanut butter). Why should the author want these details included in the passage? Yes, partially to gross you out, but probably to give some specifics about the FDA's allowance of such unpleasing items in our food. Without these details, we would only know that such allowances exist, but never have any real, powerful examples. These paragraphs are not shifting the focus to blame the FDA (F), attempting to ridicule or change the FDA's guidelines (H), or claiming that these three items have the most contaminants (J).
	19. C	WORD MEANING	The line is really reinforcing the entire passage that states insect parts in food are not only the responsibility of the kitchen preparing the final dish but could have gotten in prepared foods in a number of ways and locations.
	20. F	AUTHOR'S PURPOSE / WORD MEANING	The author seems to interrupt the flow of the passage to add his own thoughts and tone with examples like these. You know how you have a tone of voice when arguing, being sarcastic, or being sympathetic? So, imagine how the author might be speaking those little lines. That will help you determine author's tone. He seems to be saying the opposite of what the words literally mean, right? He is attempting to be *ironic* (or meaning the opposite of what one would expect). *Idealistic* (G) means, "dreaming for perfection," *malevolent* (H) means, "showing great evil or ill will." *Eloquent* (J) means, "speaking gracefully."

120

ANSWER	SKILL(S)	EXPLANATION
21. C	SUPPORTING DETAILS	The following sentence (lines 23-25) explains that fruits and vegetables are used as a substitute for the competition food because it is a healthier alternative to these typically lower calorie foods.
22. G	SUPPORTING DETAILS	The main idea of paragraph 4 (lines 51-71) is the rise of interest in competitive eating. ESPN's coverage of the hot dog eating contest (F) exposed the world to competitive eating. The tight competition of Kobayashi and Chestnut (H) has also increased interest, and Chestnut's recent successes (J) have continued to intrigue audiences. The best option for this *NOT* question is option G since Kobayashi's suspected "reversal" cannot be shown to increase popularity of the sport—it was only one part of one event.
23. C	MAIN IDEA	The article provides a history of competitive eating, including the rise in popularity and a discussion of one of the major events and its competitors. Option A about training for an eating competition is only paragraph 2's focus. Option B states that one should avoid visiting the competition in person, but the author seems to support the growing popularity, not steer people away. Though the author informs the reader of local competitions, the purpose of the article is not actually about encouraging readers to try it—it's about the history and techniques involved.
24. J	DRAWING CONCLUSIONS	Information about the "Mustard Yellow Belt" is featured in paragraph 3. The language in lines 47-50 states that Joey Chestnut "retained" the belt, which suggests that the winner of each Nathan's Hot Dog Eating Contest will get the belt. Though Chestnut did break the record (G) and has won for nine years (H), one can infer that the belt goes to the winner annually, not for these feats Chestnut has accomplished.
25. B	DRAWING CONCLUSIONS / WORD MEANING	*Regurgitation* is a fancier word for throwing up. We can infer this from the information before the word in question: "if the competitor cannot hold the amount of food filling the stomach" (lines 40-41). A *disqualification* (A) is a result of this reversal, not the meaning of the word. *Turning around* (C) seems like a similar meaning to the word *reversal*, but this meaning does not work well with the information of the paragraph. *Refusal to finish eating* (D) is not something Kobayashi did in this situation, so it would not be used to describe his close call.
26. G	AUTHOR'S PURPOSE	With this statement, the author is basically saying that this sport may not appeal to everyone. This includes the reader of the passage. We do not have any indication that the author has experienced disgusted crowds personally (H), and he does not try to exclude anyone (J) with the statement.
27. C	AUTHOR'S PURPOSE	The author wishes to explain that there are many different techniques in competitive eating, likely to show that it is much more serious and specialized than just chewing. The author may respect the competitors (B), but this doesn't seem to be why such techniques would be included based upon the information in the paragraph. Also, if used in practice only, why practice them at all? (D)
28. F	SEQUENCE	Kobayashi doubled a world record in 2001 (lines 59-60). Chestnut won his first contest in 2007 (lines 44-47), and Chestnut and Kobayashi went to overtime in 2008 (line 76-80). (Be aware of line 76 that states, "but the following year," referring to 2008).
29. A	AUTHOR'S PURPOSE	This statement is a way for the author to demonstrate that food eating competitions are not just high profile, televised events. People from all over can compete, which truly adds to the fact that contests like these exist everywhere.
30. H	DRAWING CONCLUSIONS	Since the question asks about amazing large audiences, the reader must assume that this would be when EPSN first televised the Nathan's event. Even though Kobayashi did some exciting things and stunned audiences in 2001 (G), televising the event truly brought a large audience.

121

ANSWER KEY AND EXPLANATIONS

ANSWER	SKILL(S)	EXPLANATION
31. A	SUPPORTING DETAILS / WORD MEANING	Lines 34-35 define the term in question. It explains that the combination of genes is a genotype, whereas the phenotype is how these genes create a trait that is displayed. If option C was chosen, look carefully at the phrasing. A genotype is a combination of genes from parents, not a specific, required gene for a desired trait.
32. G	MAIN IDEA	Options F, H, and J are all too specific to be the main idea. Each of these incorrect choices deals with only one portion of the passage, but option G touches upon both the major ideas of simple genetics and scientific advances that may allow alterations of some traits.
33. C	AUTHOR'S PURPOSE	The rhetorical question seems to lead the reader to answering "no," especially with the paragraph's information on the dangers a procedure like this likely include. Option A suggests that the reader is about to have such a procedure, which is very likely not true, especially if the reader is currently working on ACT practice! Option B is a bit too wide of a focus since the paragraph is only discussing an eye procedure. Option D may have been a good choice, but again, this is too wide of a focus when the paragraph only dealt with a very specific eye procedure.
34. J	SUPPORTING DETAILS	Nowhere in the passage is it suggested that melanin is something one can simply add to one's eyes in order to change appearance. Lines 2-3 show option G, paragraph 4 identifies the medical procedure to change eye color and option F, and lines 63-66 mention color contacts (option J).
35. B	SUPPORTING DETAILS	Paragraph 3 deals with dominant and recessive genes. Option A is incorrect because a dominant trait, if present, will hide a recessive trait. The way this choice is worded suggests that a recessive trait needs a dominant trait to be evident, which is exactly the opposite of what the paragraph explains. For option C, there is no evidence in the passage that states a recessive gene is responsible for changing eye color over time. Option D is excluded from possibility because of the information in lines 54-58, which states that genotypes can get much more complex than the simple eye color formula. Information to prove option B as the best choice is shown in lines 53-54.
36. G	MAIN IDEA	Lines 69-74 discuss safety as the first concern of this new procedure. Readers can tell that safety is a major concern because it is introduced first after describing the procedure, and the first idea discussed is usually the most important unless otherwise indicated.
37. A	DRAWING CONCLUSIONS	A Punnett Square needs information from both parents and can be most useful when the eye color of the parents is different. This excludes option B. A Punnett Square is not useful for parents when both have brown eyes because it is essentially a guarantee that the child will have brown eyes, so no need to use a Punnett Square! (option C) Gender is 50/50 and does not involve genes (option D). It was also not discussed in the passage if there was a way to determine gender.
38. J	DRAWING CONCLUSIONS	Since melanin is described as a dark pigment and if green and blue eyes have less melanin, (lines 21-22, 24-26) the reader can conclude that the more melanin, the darker the color. Therefore, option J remains true with skin as well in this question.
39. C	MAIN IDEA	Paragraph 2 provides basic genetic information and how things are inherited, like eye color. It does not deal with the Punnett Square (option A) like paragraph 3 does. Paragraph 3 continues to discuss heredity, so this does not serve as a divider (option B), and likewise does not divide the passage into a genetics portion and author's personal feelings portion (option D), especially since paragraph 3 still deals with genetics.
40. F	SUPPORTING DETAILS	Phenotypes are how the genes show themselves. Hair color, toe length, and teeth straightness are all visible, but brain damage is not. This is also not something one might inherit from parents but instead is a result of injury.

THANK YOU

FOR CHOOSING

FUN ACT PREP!

DID WE EARN AN A+  **?**

WE'D LOVE TO HEAR FROM YOU!

PLEASE TAKE A MOMENT TO

RATE AND REVIEW US ON

YOUR SITE OF PURCHASE

CPSIA information can be obtained
at www.ICGtesting.com
Printed in the USA
BVHW011329160721
612163BV00018B/89